TAKING CHARGE
OF
CHANGE

PAUL
SHOEMAKER

TAKING CHARGE OF CHANGE

How Rebuilders Solve Hard Problems

HarperCollins
LEADERSHIP
AN IMPRINT OF HarperCollins

Lori, my soulmate for life,
who's taught me how to lead by listening a thousand times

Sam, Nick, and Ben,
who inspire their dad to try to make them proud every day

And the thirty-eight Rebuilders in this book,
who helped me reimagine leadership for the future

Published by HarperCollins Leadership, an imprint of HarperCollins Focus LLC.

Any internet addresses, phone numbers, or company or product information printed in this book are offered as a resource and are not intended in any way to be or to imply an endorsement by HarperCollins Leadership, nor does HarperCollins Leadership vouch for the existence, content, or services of these sites, phone numbers, companies, or products beyond the life of this book.

ISBN 978-1-4002-2170-7 (eBook)
ISBN 978-1-4002-2169-1 (HC)

Library of Congress Control Number: 2020951998

Printed in the United States of America
21 22 23 LSC 10 9 8 7 6 5 4 3 2 1

CONTENTS

Our Bridges

Generosity in an Unexpected Place

Rosanne Haggerty's story goes like this—shortly after college, the building next door to where she lived in New York City was known as "Homeless Hell." The building had descended into chaos and bankruptcy and was a temporary shelter for homeless families. Also living there were two hundred longtime elderly residents and people with mental illness. The building was rife with drug selling and prostitution. She tried to interest housing groups in saving the building, but no one believed it could be transformed. Haggerty decided to leave her work and take on the mission.

Rosanne Haggerty

In 1990, she started an organization, Common Ground, to demonstrate solutions to homelessness at scale. In the following twenty years, they created nearly three thousand new homes in creatively financed buildings in and around New York City, which assisted 4,500 lower-income and homeless individuals. She also knew that homelessness was continuing to rise.

Homelessness does not discriminate by geography. It occurs from urban centers to suburbs to rural regions. Homelessness in rural settings is often "hidden," unlike the more visible street homeless in urban areas. The homelessness challenge directly affects nonprofit, public, and private sectors because of its impact on quality of life, public safety, and economic development, not to mention public health and personal endangerment.

Given that Common Ground (now named Breaking Ground) hadn't stopped homelessness from increasing, in 2011, Haggerty founded Community Solutions[1] to help communities across the United States end homelessness. Just four years later, their 100,000 Homes Campaign exceeded its goal by housing more than 105,000 Americans, a phenomenal accomplishment. Yet at the conclusion of that effort, she could not escape the stark fact that none of the communities involved had ended homelessness. She was trying to climb a mountain that kept getting steeper with a summit that kept getting higher.

If you don't know Rosanne Haggerty, at this point you might assume that because she gave it an incredibly admirable effort, doing more than just about anyone else ever had, she would feel disheartened or disgruntled. If she felt any of those feelings, it didn't stop her. In her very humble way, Rosanne Haggerty is pretty steely-eyed.

In 2015, she and Community Solutions launched Built for Zero,[2] a movement that has finally proven that, when the right conditions are met, communities can measurably end chronic and veteran homelessness (what they call functional zero). So, what is one of the hardscrabble, on-the-street, bare-knuckles keys to finally making progress on one of America's most visible, gritty, and seemingly intractable problems? In her own words, a *Generosity Mindset*.

How do you end chronic homelessness in eleven communities across America, like Arlington, Virginia; Riverside, California; and Chattanooga, Tennessee? And how do you end veteran homelessness in Bergen County, New Jersey; Lancaster, Pennsylvania; and Rockford, Illinois?

Apparently by

- creating a commitment to unity and looking for what you can commonly share while respecting one another's differences;
- leaving room for multiple points of view; and
- finding your edge of discomfort as a leader, just as a rock climber does, pushing beyond your percieved boundaries in order to lead diverse people.

And by doing all these things, a city will "be in relationship around a shared, nonpartisan community goal" and you will create a "powerful shared truth, like knowing the names and identities of each homeless person," so it's personal to everyone. That's what a Generosity Mindset looks like, and that's how to fight one of the most complex, perplexing civic challenges in America. Haggerty can hold that generosity even in the midst of such complexity.

I've hung out in quite a few meetings and conversations with her over the last few years. I don't know that I would have understood what a Generosity Mindset meant when I first met her. Over time, it became more and more clear. She believes in and is looking for others who believe with her. She keeps an even keel at all times; that's her makeup. She leads by bringing everyone in and making sure the work moves at the speed of trust. And she leads through a strategically and intentionally generous mindset.

Haggerty has accrued just about every award and fellowship you possibly could in the social sector. She is also an exemplar of a new kind of leader America will need more and more of in our future, starting right now. She's a *Rebuilder*.

The Bridge in the Park behind My House

When I was in first and second grade, growing up in Fort Dodge, Iowa, Snell-Crawford Park was just a few hundred feet from our backyard. In the hot, humid summers, I'd take off into the woods, try to avoid the poison ivy, and walk along Soldier Creek. Somewhere along the trail was a small, simple arch bridge with a road running over the creek. I'd sit underneath that bridge and wait for cars to go rumbling over. Even with a bridge that simple, I was sort of fascinated by how a structure could hold up a whole concrete street with cars speeding across.

Bridges across the United States in 2020 are deteriorating. A recent report[3] estimates that it will take more than eighty years to fix all of them. There are more than 600,000 bridges in America, and 235,000 of them need some sort of repair. That's almost 40 percent. Nearly 8 percent, 46,000 are "structurally deficient" and in need of urgent rebuilding.

The state of our deteriorating, structurally deficient bridges in 2020 is an evocative metaphor for the nation we are living in right now. The social, economic, and health structures underlying

American civil society[4] are in a more critical condition than they have been in decades.

Some parts of our nation need urgent repair and rebuilding, like that 8 percent of bridges that are structurally deficient. Perhaps no issue so visibly reflects our nation's need for rebuilding as homelessness, the work to which Rosanne Haggerty has dedicated her life. As is and always will be the case, these times call for a new kind of leader.

Haggerty, and the other thirty-six leaders you'll read about, is a Rebuilder, a leader for the 2020s. Rebuilders have a combination of qualities and skill sets that will enable them to effectively address the accelerating economic, social, and health disparities across an increasingly uneven, siloed America.

The Five Vital Traits of Rebuilders

Those five leadership qualities and skill sets, the five vital traits, of Rebuilders that will matter the most are:

1. 24-7 Authenticity
2. Complexity Capacity
3. Generosity Mindset
4. Data Conviction
5. Cross-Sector Fluency

These traits are, like the parts of a bridge, interrelated and form a cohesive whole. When we walk or drive across any bridge, unless you're an engineer, you may not fully grasp how many connected parts—piles, piers, abutments, superstructure, and so on—work together.

A bridge stays in place because all the forces acting on it are in balance. Most bridges stand for years, decades, even centuries.

There are many kinds of bridges, but virtually all of them carefully balance two main forces: compression (a pushing or squeezing force, acting inward) and tension (a pulling or stretching force, acting outward).[5]

For Rebuilders, the the vital traits of 24-7 Authenticity and a Generosity Mindset are in balance with the tangible skill sets of Data Conviction and the Capacity for Complexity. And the trait that connects them together is Cross-Sector Fluency (see Figure I.1). We'll dive much deeper into all five traits in Part III.

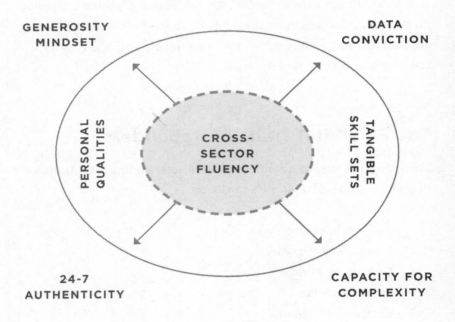

FIGURE I.1

This book is for socially conscious and civically active leaders who are starting to redefine the leader they need to be and are hungry for clarity, stories, and direction. These five connected traits give you, your teams, and your organization an indispensable checklist for effective leadership for the 2020s.

Why These Five Traits

Over the course of 2019, I took time piecing together a holistic picture of America's economic, social, and health conditions. It became quickly apparent that these stark disparities are weakening our nation just as our bridges are weakening. They are creating a scale and scope of change unlike anything we have seen in generations. I'll paint that picture in more detail in Part II.

Eventually, I came to understand that those underlying economic, health, and social disparities are like a faulty bridge structure. They have helped create and are playing out in the context of five megachallenges America is facing in the decade ahead:

1. Significant, growing differences in the access to and use of technology combined with the hyper attention of today's media as major amplifiers of our inequities.
2. A breadth and depth of challenges greater than we've faced in the last seventy-five years, especially now in a post(?)-COVID world.
3. The reality that we are less connected and more siloed, making coming together harder today than it has perhaps ever been.
4. Slowing, less certain, more unequal progress across a broad array of social, health, and economic indicators.
5. The intersecting and blurring of lines between historical norms of our private, nonprofit, and public sectors in ways we have never seen before (and it isn't going back to the way it was).

These five megachallenges directly suggest the five vital traits desperately needed in the leaders who will make the difference in the decade ahead.

MEGACHALLENGE	REBUILDER VITAL TRAIT
Unequal acesss to technology and hyper-media as amplifiers	24-7 Authenticity
Breadth & depth of challenges greatest in seventy-five years	Complexity Capacity
Less connected and more siloed than perhaps ever been	Generosity Mindset
Slowing, less certain, more unequal progress	Data Conviction
Blurring lines between private, nonprofit, and public sectors	Cross-Sector Fluency

The best way to stress test my thinking about those five challenges-to-traits connections was having conversations with dozens of leaders, like Rosanne Haggerty, who are coming up with some of the most effective solutions today that address these disparities. My conclusions in my review of these megachallenges as well as my talks brought me back to the realization that these five traits are key to leadership in the 2020s.

The meat of this book consists of stories of people who have led real change and are exemplars of those five vital traits. They are leaders who are taking charge of all this change. Many of them aren't famous, widely known names; they are akin to the Level 5 leaders Jim Collins unearthed in *Good to Great*.[6] Yet all these Rebuilders are true leaders in their own way.

Looking into the Future

To be clear, *my point of view is prospective, not retrospective*. My belief in the centrality of these five traits of Rebuilders as keys to our future is based on objective and extensive observation and experience. It is not based on retrospective science.

The aspiration of this book is to see the complex challenges facing us in the future and the unique traits leaders will need to effectively respond. Just as our deteriorating bridges will require significant resources and commitment before they can be repaired or rebuilt, America will require a unique generation of leaders to truly begin to repair and rebuild our civil society.

How to Use This Book

In Part I, you will learn about three more of these Rebuilders and their stories and traits. I'll explain more about how I studied and learned in order to arrive at my leadership perspective. We'll also examine the generosity-complexity and authenticity-data dyads.

The arc of America over the last seventy, especially the last twenty, years is the backdrop we'll walk through in Part II. We made significant, albeit at times unequal, progress between the end of World War II and the turn of the millennium. If one looks at measures of economic, social, or health progress, the general trend line was positive progress for most of the fifty years after the war. That's *where we came from,* but *where we are today,* the challenges facing us in 2020, are radically different than those we faced twenty, even ten, years ago.

Today we are at a critical juncture, with America becoming much more unequal and siloed. We have "amplifiers" that accelerate and exacerbate those trends. Ultimately, we have to ask, "Where are we going?" Leadership can be a decisive, maybe the most decisive, force to lead American communities and companies to a better future.

The skill sets, qualities, and traits it takes to *rebuild* are different from what it takes to build, and that is what we will dive deeper into in Part III. There are always new products to build, organizations to create, and causes to attack. In the decade ahead, the traits of leaders as Rebuilders will be even more important to American civil society than the builders. We will define and describe in-depth the five vital traits of leadership it will take to rebuild an America that has become far too unequal and siloed in the 2020s. And you'll meet thirty-two more Rebuilders.

Here are a few lenses to use as you think about the five traits:

▶ As an individual leader—what leadership muscle do I need to build or strengthen?
▶ As a team—what qualities and skill sets are missing or do we need to build together?
▶ As an organization or company—what kind of leaders and traits exist up and down the organization? How are we making sure the right leadership is distributed, vertically and horizontally, across our org chart?
▶ As a neighborhood or community—if we are going to truly help solve problems in our place in the world, do we have the right mix of citizens and local leaders?

I'll bring those traits together in three brief case studies in Part IV—one retrospective, one current, and a third prospective, aspirational scenario. I want to present some real-world applications of how these leaders and their vital traits come together as a whole, not just the parts, to create change. We'll look at failures as well as successes.

And in Part V, I want to be clear that I am worried about America in the dark of night but fundamentally optimistic in the light of day. We do live in a much more unequal, siloed, and fractured America than any of us could have envisioned just one generation ago. At the end of the day, we have to get this right for America and the world. There are major implications for all three sectors of our economy: private, public, and nonprofit. It's about whether we should be fundamentally optimistic or pessimistic about where the American experiment is going, because it's not nearly as obvious as it used to be. And in conclusion, you'll meet one last Rebuilder.

Massive Problem versus Generational Opportunity

America is at a looming inflection point. COVID has brought us even more abruptly to a massive reset moment, for America and for leadership. And that reset got accelerated and expanded by the sickening murder of George Floyd and the social movement it reignited. Like all change, our times are not only cause for uncertainty but opportunities for new leaders to step forward. Leaders ready for this century, not the year 2000 version, but for the 2020s and beyond. The previous twenty years might as well have been equivalent to a century full of change that we are still trying to catch up to.

Massive upheavals like 2020 can be moments for undoing and expelling old ways of thinking and working and being. As Seth Godin articulated recently in his typically simple yet powerful language, "The industrial era, struggling for the last decade or two, is now officially being replaced by one based on connection and leadership and the opportunity to show up and make a difference."[7] This is where Rebuilders come in, as powerful forces for a new kind of connection and leadership. For a future that otherwise risks fast becoming less and less equal and more and more siloed along economic, political, and health lines.

To be blunt, there are heroes and villains to be made in the years ahead, just as there have been at other huge inflection points in American history. From the robber barons at the turn of the twentieth century and war profiteers during the World Wars to the courage of the greatest generation and the frontline heroes of both 9/11 and COVID, American history is replete with villains and heroes. In times like these, leadership is the seminal lever in civil society. Those who show up with the five vital traits will not only be the Rebuilders for the future, they will be genuine American heroes.

Taking Charge of Change speaks directly to a powerful truth: Each of us does not have to passively let change happen to us. We can each be a leader that shapes change and creates the kind of change we want to see in our world as a Rebuilder. We can't control all of the change around us, but we can be an active positive force in leading how it will play out in the decade ahead for our communities, companies, and citizens.

If we can bring forward truly new and better leaders, then this period of time we are in will turn out to be a moment not just of division and inequity in the near term but of progress toward stronger, better communities and companies over the long term.

The Rebuilders you read about will give you belief and hope. They are doing the work now to strengthen and rebuild our economic, social, and health bridges across America, but we need a lot more like them. Leaders like you.

The times we live in call for renovation as much or more than innovation. There will always be entrepreneurs driving for the new and the never-been-done-before. But we will need to lean in more in the decade ahead on rebuilding, making more with what we have. We need reinvention as much as invention. And it will all have to happen in a post-COVID America that will be far more resource constrained.

The decade ahead will be The Decade of the Rebuilders.

TAKING CHARGE OF CHANGE

PART ONE

Our Rebuilders

Getting Excited about Garbage

If I didn't know better, I'd swear I was watching ESPN's *SportsCenter*, with all the gyrations and exuberance of one of their data analysts. He was waving his hands around, with high energy in his voice. He must have been explaining the trajectory of a Sue Bird three-pointer.

Felipe Moreno

Or the geometry and foot speed of LeBron James running full court to impossibly block a shot in the closing seconds to help Cleveland secure its first NBA title.[1] But in fact, his excitement was about . . . drum roll . . . the results of waste and recycling management in Phoenix, Arizona.

Felipe Moreno is the deputy director of Public Works for the City of Phoenix. More to the point, he is a leader of the people around him—his staff, the men and women who operate the garbage and recycling trucks. He couldn't be the genuine, forward-looking leader he is without a passion for and a *conviction about data.*

In the last five years, Phoenix's waste diversion rate jumped from 16 percent in 2014 to 34 percent in 2019. This is significant data, which Moreno likes to point out. Why? Because unlike many cities with mandates and legislation requiring waste diversion, Phoenix has always had a voluntary recycling and waste diversion program.

Public sector entities often find it very hard to show measurable impact. In the case of Phoenix, data has become a core part of telling its sustainability story—from routing efficiencies to waste tonnage and recycling challenges that lead to diversion solutions. Generally, citizens (i.e., voters) are constantly frustrated with the inefficiency and bureaucracy of their local and state governments (sometimes rightfully so). But Moreno can tell a clear data story. You can listen to him on a podcast featuring great business minds and thought leaders talking about his excitement for waste management![2]

Moreno told me data isn't just *tactical,* which seems obvious with numbers; sometimes it's *strategic.* Ultimately, it's a core tool of leadership. These are some of the tangible ways in which Moreno's Data Conviction enables him to be a more effective leader:

He didn't come up through the ranks as a garbage truck driver; he didn't walk into his role with that street cred. Data is an indispensable part of how he establishes his leadership credibility "on the street" (literally).

It guides his decisions on the people he needs to hire, including some he calls "hybrid" management. They have to be able to translate from the data to human beings and back, constantly and effectively.

One of his leadership strategies is to be authentic and vulnerable about what he doesn't know (because he didn't drive a truck) but bring the incremental value of what he does know. There is a natural connection between his conviction about the data and his genuine authenticity. His leadership equation is data + authenticity = leadership.

One of the fascinating, unexpected parts of his leadership story is his background. He's not a public works major or a policy wonk or a statistics nerd. Moreno is a social worker by education and by mindset. One of the qualities you will see across many of these Rebuilders is they often didn't come up through the usual, traditional pathways. That different pathway is, in fact, a real strength that brings diversity and new perspectives to solving our challenges in the decade ahead.

Data, and leaders with conviction about it, has become a whole new platform for change in the nonprofit and public sectors, especially. The private sector has always had the one bottom line, net profit. The other two sectors haven't had nearly that clarity, but now, by embracing data, they can take significant steps toward a stronger, more objective platform for community leadership.

Moreno has helped build a culture of data, along with the city manager, Ed Zuercher (who has his own data story for the whole city).[3] A culture that doesn't just embrace data but empowers people though the data. A culture that values data but doesn't allow the numbers to dehumanize the work or the people. And a culture that doesn't assume the way we've always done things in the past is the right way going forward.

Today, Moreno is doing what really great leaders do: expanding the leadership pool down through the organization, in part by creating the first apprenticeship program in the nation for municipal solid waste equipment operators (SWEO),[4] that is, garbage truck drivers. Rebecca Estrada is one of seven apprentices who just graduated and says she feels like she's breaking barriers. "I'm loving the challenge of driving around a big truck and serving our community," she says. "I want to be an inspiration to other women and to my kids that we can do whatever we want to do."

One of our subthemes about Rebuilders in the decade ahead is that we need leaders at all levels of organizations and communities, including in lots of unexpected and nontraditional places. The City of Phoenix now has more and more new leaders driving all over the streets of Phoenix every day on every block. They just happen to be garbage truck drivers, too.

From the Bridge Tower

A bridge tender sits in the tower alongside a drawbridge. There are four of them around my hometown of the last thirty years, Seattle. The bridge tender operates the bridge to ensure the safe passage of water traffic under, and vehicle traffic over, the bridge. There is nothing particularly omniscient about the bridge tenders' perspectives, but they do see through a wide-angle lens on the comings and goings around that bridge.

When I first started working on this book in the summer of 2019, I took a wide-angle focus, looking for stories and best practices of economic and social change across all sectors, geographies, and demographics of America. As I was looking into those examples of positive change, against the backdrop of our megachallenges, my focus started to shift—not just looking at the facts and strategies about the change, but instead at the people and leaders behind those changes.

The conversations with those leaders making real change elucidated a definable, distinct set of traits that consistently showed up. My primary focus shifted toward the kind of leaders and leadership our nation needs to create that positive change. Simply put, I let the data and research, and especially what I learned from dozens of leaders, tell me what to focus on.

I had a preconceived notion of what I *wanted* to write about. Over time, I discovered what I *should* write about.

How and Whom I Studied

Five years ago, I wrote *Can't Not Do: The Compelling Social Drive That Changes Our World* (Wiley).[5] The hope was to provide a road map for citizens, philanthropists, and volunteers who wanted to make a bigger difference in their world and in their own lives.

This time I am trying to bring together what I've learned in thirty-five years working across all three sectors and offer a perspective and guideposts for leaders who know that a new form of leadership is needed. Throughout the last year of writing, there have been a lot of tables, Excel graphs, Venn diagrams, word clouds, and so on.

I studied dozens of leaders from all three sectors: private, public, and nonprofit. I looked at a broad range of industries and causes, and leaders with a diverse set of backgrounds and worldviews. I started with leaders I knew personally and did outreach through my network of trusted friends to add to the list.

I strove for a mix of people from each of the sectors, as well as different genders, ethnicities, and places in companies and communities—a mix like the collective profile of leaders America is absolutely going to need in the 2020s. The leaders I focused on meet the criteria below. Imperfect, but intentional. Subjective, but substantiated.

- ▶ They have achieved a level of measurable success or effectiveness. There is some objective, public measure by which one can ascertain effectiveness, which usually note in their stories.
- ▶ A majority of them have substantial experience in two, or all three, sectors of the American economy.
- ▶ Each clearly demonstrated and is an exemplar of a specific trait (or two) that fits the profile of a Rebuilder.

One of the interesting twists is where the lessons come from. For a long time now, sometimes correctly and sometimes arrogantly, the working assumption is that nonprofit leaders could learn from how private sector leaders work. Looking ahead, I think we've crossed over to a world where the leadership lessons from the nonprofit (and public) sector are equally as instructive to private sector leaders.

We just saw it above: the private sector has always had the one bottom line, the guidepost of net profit. The other two sectors haven't had nearly that clarity. But now private sector leaders cannot, increasingly by their own choice, just look at net profit as the one indicator of success and call it a day (see the Profit and Purpose section in chapter 9). Leaders who know how to navigate greater ambiguity and complexity of goals become more and more valuable. Those leaders are out there. If the private sector is smart, they will start recruiting more of them now. Nonprofit and public sector leaders are used to the complexity of not having the clarity of one bottom line.

The learning is across and between all three sectors as never before. For a long time, nonprofits have had to work with the private sector for their financial and human capital and the public sector for its unique scale of resources. They know how to be bridge builders already. Now private sector leaders need to have just as much Cross-Sector Fluency. They can't just stick their heads out of their for-profit silos once in a while for episodic interactions; they are in all three sectors constantly. And the public sector needs to learn how to effectively leverage and convene all three sectors together if they want to have a chance of realizing their civic aspirations.

Are Current Leadership Models Broken?

Rebuilders are leaders who don't look and sound and act the same as we are used to seeing. Qualities like hyperauthenticity, an exceptional capacity for complexity, extensive cross-sector experience, plus others are what will define the leaders we need for our future.

Some leadership qualities are timeless, some are temporal. For example, *The Ajax Dilemma* by Paul Woodruff is about timeless qualities in leadership, going back to ancient Greece. Jim Collins does some of the best, intentional, deep work on Level 5 leaders in *Good to Great*. Bob Johansen's *Leadership Literacies* posits combinations of disciplines, practices, and worldviews that will be needed to thrive in a volatile, uncertain, complex, and ambiguous (VUCA)[6] world.

This isn't about repudiating earlier leadership models, it's about the future and what's needed now. What I'm suggesting is that there are (1) timeless leadership qualities that get called on differently in a new age and (2) altogether new attributes that are more needed in this decade ahead. A different world takes different leaders with different traits.

Living Oliver Wendell Holmes's Quote

When COVID hit and really sunk in across the world in March 2020, it was a month none of us will ever forget. One of the most important and complex events that followed in April was the distribution of $2.2 trillion in federal funds in a nanosecond (CARES Act). Critical, vital, and insanely complex. There had to have been tens of thousands of corporate lobbyists and special interests trying to both direct and obtain as much of that funding as possible.

Dan Cardinali

What if you were one of the much smaller number of leaders responsible for watching out for the nonprofit sector (which represents nearly 10 percent of the American workforce)? And you had exponentially fewer resources to invest in lobbying and advocacy, compared with corporate America? You were essentially trying to grab a few needles (i.e., resources) in a massive, $2 trillion haystack that was constantly moving. One of the key leaders for the sector was Dan Cardinali, CEO of the Independent Sector.[7]

Cardinali was someone already world-class at dealing with complexity. I knew that from being a colleague for ten-plus years. I wondered how you navigate a complex morass like the CARES Act and the hundreds of other challenges he's dealt with over the years. Most of us have seen (and probably misquoted) the brilliant quote, attributed to Holmes: "For the simplicity on this side of complexity, I wouldn't give you a fig. But for the simplicity on the other side of complexity, for that I would give you anything I have."[8] Cardinali says that simplicity on the other side is a "set of clear values that he constantly applies":

> Put human beings at the center of everything.
> Strive for people to thrive, not just survive.
> Focus most on those on the margin.

I wrote down those notes from our conversation and didn't think much about the list. When I went back a few days later and reread the list, I just sat for a few moments with the power of those simple values. It was profoundly clear to me how a leader like Cardinali has the immense *capacity for complexity* that he does. He finds the clarity amid the complexity because he has a North Star. The values that guide him are as clear to him as the world is murky and complex around him.

Like many of the exemplars whose stories are being shared, Cardinali exemplifies more than one vital trait. In his case, he is also cross-sector fluent (trait 5) as well. Independent Sector is, by definition, an organization created to live at the intersection of complexity, at the crossover of the three sectors.

Before Independent Sector, Dan Cardinali was president of Communities in Schools (CIS),[9] the nation's largest dropout prevention organization, with operations in twenty-six states and the District of Columbia. CIS serves more than 1.5 million of America's most disenfranchised students. Under Cardinali's leadership, the organization developed and embraced an evidence-based model of integrated student service provision. Among the students that were case-managed by CIS, 99 percent stayed in school, 88 percent improved their academics, and 91 percent graduated or received a GED.

There are two other vitally important aspects of complexity in 2020 that a Rebuilder like Cardinali elucidates: (1) the costs of *not* dealing with it, and (2) whether you can *distribute* that capacity among a leadership team. When it comes to leaders who do not deal well with complexity, we've all been around ones who got to where they are because they stuck to a tried-and-true playbook that becomes increasingly irrelevant. Ignoring the accelerating complexity around them, some leaders keep working decisions at a tactical-and-too-simplistic level based on the past reality. They sacrifice working strategically based on future-facing, more complex conditions. The challenges grow and the old solutions no longer take root.

One of Cardinali's favorite types of musicians are jazz pianists, an artful metaphor for the capacity for complexity. The best jazz pianists are both technically good and creatively agile. Metaphorically, we have a lot of existing leaders who are technically proficient today but not agile enough for tomorrow's complexity. They are still playing the same old tunes in the same old way. Technical proficiency will usually be necessary, but it's almost always insufficient.

Finally, Cardinali and I exchanged notes on whether a leader can share or distribute her or his capacity for complexity to a team. The truth is that it's hard to do. That may not be an answer that feels politically correct, but it's largely true. Some Rebuilders have a learned or innate capacity for complexity, but it often doesn't work well when delegated.

That capacity is not a particularly common trait, so it's better to hold that in a leader. Make sure, however, that there are a range of perspectives and other traits among the team members. The team can handle complexity collectively, but don't assume it's a trait that is easily transferred to other individuals.

I've been in many meetings and conversations with Cardinali. When he's in the room (or on Zoom), he always brings a clarity and sharpness to his perspective. There are no wasted words and there is always incremental value added. He truly knows how to find and articulate that simplicity on the other side of complexity. I don't know many people I can say that so clearly about.

Generosity-Complexity and Authenticity-Data Pairs

We already see that these five traits are not random or disconnected. Let's take it a step further and look at two combinations of traits. The Generosity-Complexity and Authenticity-Data dyads (see visual again, page xii) showed up time and time again with these leaders. Not universally, but they showed up empirically and much more often than not. These complementary and strong pairs of traits are like the many parts of a bridge that reinforce and keep other parts in balance.

Once you read enough of the leaders' stories, like those of Rosanne Haggerty, Felipe Moreno, Dan Cardinali, and Trish Millines, seeing these pairings will start to be second nature. Perhaps these combinations can be another construct you can adopt as part of your personal framework for leadership:

▶ A Generosity Mindset needs to be able to process Complexity in order to know where and how opportunities and connections arise that can be leveraged and sustained.

▶ Complexity Capacity needs heart and a Generosity Mindset to put that intricate understanding to work with and for real people.

▶ Data Conviction risks being dehumanizing or too formulaic without the genuine quality of 24-7 Authenticity.

▶ The trust built by 24-7 Authenticity is ideally paired with the Data Conviction and facts that can back it up.

▶ And Cross-Sector Fluency is often the bridging, integrating trait that can bring the right people, ideas, and solutions to the table together.

Finding It Inside Yourself
When Someone Finally Sees It in You

Today, Trish Millines is an author, has appeared on *Oprah*, and is known as a pioneer for women of color in the tech sector. Probably most important of all (other than raising four great kids with her partner), she cofounded the Technology Access Foundation (TAF).[10] TAF works with public education to create access to transformative systems of learning for students and teachers of color to eliminate

race-based disparities. She is a national-level leader who speaks for access for kids of color. But it wasn't always "easy" for Trish.

Millines put herself through college. She was the first in her family to go to college and landed the first full women's basketball scholarship to Monmouth College. When Millines first started in the software world in the '80s, her earliest challenges weren't just

Trish Millines

navigating this new world called software. She was trying to survive the systemic sexism and racism she ran into every day. At that early stage of her career, she was just "surviving," in her own words.

Millines continued to just survive until she finally found a manager, at Fortune Systems in San Francisco, that was a giver, not a taker, and asked her to be herself. A mentor created the conditions for her authenticity to begin to flourish.

She navigated her way from Fortune Systems, where she wrote software to test missile systems, to Microsoft in the '90s. After working as a software tester for several years, eventually she became the first chief diversity officer at Microsoft. That was well before such a position became more common and, today, more strategic (not just in the HR department), in more and more corporations.

Over the next decade of tremendous growth at Microsoft, Millines saw little change in the culture of the high-tech industry. Women and people of color remained grossly underrepresented. After careful research she traced the root of the problem to the lack of access to rigorous, relevant technology training in our public schools, particularly those in traditionally underserved communities of color. Like Rosanne Haggerty, she had to confront a reality that not nearly enough progress was being made.

She had a choice. Maybe she had a dream to climb the corporate ladder. But if she was being truly authentic, facing reality as it was, not as she wished it were, she couldn't stay where she was (see Michael McAfee on page 72, too). She made the choice that wasn't as easy and certainly not as lucrative.

She left Microsoft in 1996 and founded TAF. In its more than twenty-three-year history, TAF has impacted more than 19,600 students resulting in a 99 percent on-time high school graduation rate and a 100 percent college acceptance rate. That's one hell of a bottom line, no matter what sector you work in. Millines is as data driven as she is kid driven.

Millines is one of the most what-you-see-is-what-you-get people I've ever known. She is the kind of truth-to-power leader with 24-7 Authenticity that can have (a) the guts to say hard things out loud, and (b) everyone in the room respect her words. That kind of authenticity buys you the ability to speak up when others can't and to lead when others won't. In a deeply divided and siloed America, Rebuilders like Trish Millines have a reservoir of trust they have gained through authenticity. They can and will spend that trust capital to make their communities stronger.

Millines became a trailblazer for equity and kids of color in the tech world, but getting there was not an easy road. Her authenticity carried her through the challenges and choices. Trish herself has today become the person that many others "call on for the truth." The once mentee has become the mentor, and a powerful one. She is now willing and able to say what should be said. Not because she knows it will benefit her in some way but because it needs to be said.

Maybe as much as any one leader you will read about, Trish Millines possesses all five of those Rebuilder traits. I'm sure she'd deny that, but if you look at the qualities and skill sets she brings to her work, combined with her career experience directly in and working side by side with all three sectors, you'll see what I mean.

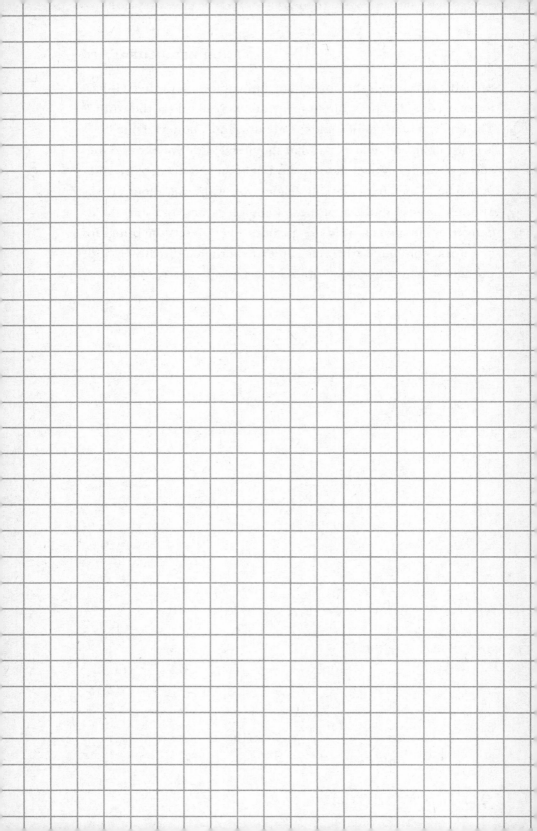

PART TWO

Why Rebuilders Matter for the 2020s

Back to the Bridge behind My House

A few times when I got back from my walks through the park and under the bridge in Snell-Crawford Park, I remember looking through an old, well-worn book about bridges. They are some pretty amazing structures understandable at a simple level and consisting of three basic parts: (1) the superstructure, the portion of the structure above water (or above another road or railway) that is the span that directly receives the load; (2) the substructure, that middle connecting layer that includes the abutments and piers; and (3) the foundation, which includes the piles and underlying structure on top of which everything rests.[1]

The foundation comprises the elements—the piles and caps—that connect the structure to the earth and transfer loads from it to the ground below. Just like those piles and pile caps on deteriorating bridges, the economic, social, and health foundations of America are in great need of repair and rebuilding. Just like any bridge you

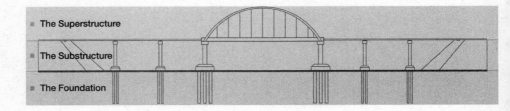

The Superstructure

The Substructure

The Foundation

drive or walk or bike across, our nation is only as strong as the underlying foundation.

Human beings are always trying to "build bridges" with people they might disagree with. Dozens of songs include the word *bridge* in the title, maybe most famously "Bridge over Troubled Water." Perhaps the most poignant bridge metaphor is of providing a crossing to the hereafter.

Bridges do, in fact, have to be rebuilt across American civil society in the decade ahead. Not just the physical ones. We need to:

- ▶ Rebuild economic bridges for more Americans to be able to get back to the middle class and to have a chance again at the American dream.
- ▶ Create technology bridges so that access to broadband and enhanced (not just basic) technology is greater and can narrow the gap between the haves and have-nots.
- ▶ Have leaders that know how to bridge from the private to the nonprofit to the public sector.
- ▶ Make real, sustained progress on many more "bridges" that need to be rebuilt across American civil society.

As you read about these *individual* leaders and their vital traits, I hope you will also think about the *collective* whole of leadership we need. We need lots of these individuals, but we also need collective teams and organizations full of them. You won't often find all of these traits in one person (occasionally you will), but there is no doubt we can build a movement of leaders that can come together.

Many of these Rebuilders have already been leading, as you'll read, but we need to more intentionally connect more like them together in the 2020s. Just like you can't build a fully functioning, beautiful bridge without all the parts, we can't make the change we want to see without all of the traits of these Rebuilders being brought together and working together, like the many parts of a strong, enduring bridge.

To understand *where we are today* and the weakened foundation upon which our future sits, and *where we're going*, we need to first look back at *where we have come from*.

CHAPTER ONE

Where We've Come From (1950-2000)

I n many ways, the successful expansion and sophistication of bridges across the United States in the half century after World War II, when more than two-thirds of our bridges have been built, mirrored the economic, social, and health progress of America during that same time. The story of America, from 1950 to 2000, was one of progress on a range of challenges that affect us all—childhood mortality, literacy, life expectancy, public health, women's and civil rights, per capita GDP, and the list goes on. The United States made it through two world wars in the first half of the 1900s and subsequently led, and greatly benefited from, the global recovery coming out of World War II.

▶ ▶ ▶

Economic, 1950–2000

Progress wasn't always even, but overall, there was steadily growing economic prosperity (technically, as measured by real GDP per capita) in the second half of the twentieth century. For a long time, this progress broadened the middle class, fueled our economy, and brought a significant majority of citizens along.

If we look at the '50s, '60s, '70s, and well into the '80s, we see growth and we see it at similar levels across most (not all) income and wealth brackets. Americans not only were prospering, but they were doing so largely evenly, which is certainly one prescription for a thriving middle class and a healthy civil society.[1] As Figure 1.1 shows, the bars for each income bracket are largely even from 1950 to 1980 (but then in the '80s, they started to become increasingly uneven, which we'll talk about in chapter 2).

Average Annual Change in Mean Family Income, 1950–2010, by Quintile and for the Top 5 Percent

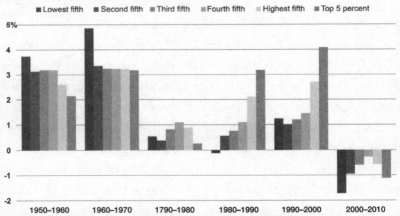

Source: US Census Bureau, Historical Income Tables, Table F-3 for 1966 to 2010, and derived from Tables F-2 and F-7 for 1950 to 1965. Download from http://www.census.gov/hhes/www/income/data/historical/families on July 11, 2012.
PEW RESEARCH CENTER

FIGURE 1.1

Health, 1950–2000

There was a strong sense of significant advances in health, benefiting citizens similarly and broadly, between 1950 and 2000. Maybe the broadest, most comprehensive, all-encompassing indicator of improving health is average life expectancy. Over those fifty years, Americans' life expectancy progressed from a little more than sixty-one years to more than seventy-seven (see Figure 1.2).[2]

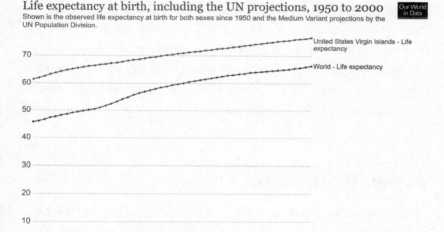

Life expectancy at birth, including the UN projections, 1950 to 2000
Shown is the observed life expectancy at birth for both sexes since 1950 and the Medium Variant projections by the UN Population Division.

United States Virgin Islands - Life expectancy

World - Life expectancy

Source: UN Population Division (2017 Revision)   OurWorldInData.org/future-population-growth/ • CC BY

FIGURE 1.2

There was a long list of health advances[3] that Americans commonly benefited from, including these:

▶ **1952:** The first cardiac pacemaker to control irregular heartbeat is developed.
▶ **1955:** Jonas Salk develops the first polio vaccine.
▶ **1964:** The first vaccine for measles is developed (with one for mumps coming a few years after that).

▶ **1965:** Medicare and Medicaid are introduced to the US health-care system for senior citizens and the poor.

▶ **1980:** The WHO (World Health Organization) announces smallpox has been eradicated.

▶ **1982:** The Jarvik-7 artificial heart is implanted in patient Barney Clark. He lived 112 days.

▶ **1983:** Scientists identify HIV, the virus that causes AIDS.

▶ **1992:** The first vaccine for hepatitis A is created.

We capped off the century with scientists at the Human Genome Project releasing a draft of the human genome to the public. For the first time, the world could read the complete set of human genetic information and begin to discover what our twenty-three thousand genes do. The associated potential for making progress on or solving major public health problems felt so imminent and prominent.

Social, 1950–2000

Social progress is defined as the capacity of a society to meet the basic human needs of its citizens, establish the building blocks that allow citizens and communities to enhance and sustain the quality of their lives, and create the conditions for *all individuals to reach their full potential.* That is an aspiration we can all agree upon. Progress in the social sector imperfectly lends itself to hard data. As much as any dimension of American society between 1950 and 2000, social progress is harder to see as a straight line. But there was progress in women's rights, civil rights, the rights of disabled people, gay rights, and so on.

Just more than a hundred years ago, women didn't have the right to vote. At the 1964 Republican convention, Margaret Chase Smith became the first woman to have her name placed in nomination for the presidency at a major political party's convention. At the press conference[4] at which she announced her decision, there was frequent laughter and dismissiveness toward her candidacy. Shirley Chisholm was the first black woman elected to the US Congress in 1968 and was a candidate for president in 1972. Geraldine Ferrero was the vice-presidential nominee in 1984. Political candidacy is only one way to measure social progress, of course, but it is symbolically relevant and translates to other ways in which women made progress.

The participation rate of women in the workforce grew steadily in the second half of the 1900s (see Figure 1.3). Barely sixty years ago, women in professional roles was still an emergent, not yet socially acceptable pattern in the modern life of companies and families. Over the subsequent thirty years, there were major strides forward, though clearly there is still much progress to be made.

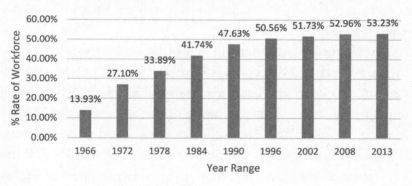

US Participation Rates for Women Professionals 1966–2013
Source: US Equal Employment Opportunities Commission 2013

FIGURE 1.3

Don't take my (a man's) word for it.

You could make a case that, along with the tech revolution, the most provocative upending destabilizing thrilling change in the course of human history is that we're finally in it. . . . We're here now, women are in the world, and we will not be bullied.[5]   —Meryl Streep

As you move up, as you engage more and more people in the company and take on broader roles, this idea of "looking the part" becomes more and more of a challenge when you don't look the part. But there's nothing I can do, or wanted to do, about being a black female. I like both of those things. At the end of the day, the people who were around me had to do a little bit more adjusting than I did.

—URSULA BURNS,

former CEO and chairperson, Xerox

(the first black woman to lead a Fortune 500 company)

In 1954, state-sponsored segregation of public schools was declared unconstitutional by the US Supreme Court in the landmark case *Brown v. the Board of Education*. It took many years to implement this decision, and it is certainly very much a work in progress to this day. It was intended to create equal access to quality education for all of our children and youth. In the second half of the twentieth century, one could point to progress, not nearly sufficient and not even, but nevertheless real.

The National Assessment of Educational Progress (NAEP) is the largest nationally representative assessment of what America's students know and learn in various subject areas. There was a much-too-slow yet steady narrowing of the achievement scores in reading, across all age groups, between black and white students. It began in the '70s and continued even into the first years of the twenty-first century. Over that thirty-five-year period, the size of that gap (between the upper and lower lines) on reading scores, across grade levels, decreased by 30 to 50 percent (see Figure 1.4).

The passage of the Civil Rights Act in 1964 and the Voting Rights Act of 1965 were watershed moments of social progress for people of color, especially African Americans. Progress was very choppy, the civil unrest in the '50s and '60s and violence against black people was appalling, but the broadest trend line was positive on these critical social challenges. As Martin Luther King Jr. said, "The arc of the moral universe is long, but it bends towards justice."

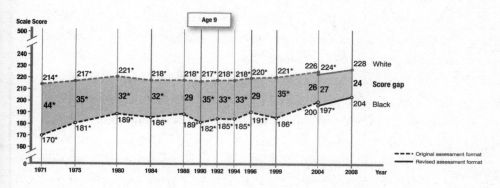

FIGURE 1.4

"There Is No NAZ without Data"

There are many ways in which Sondra Samuels embodies that social progress through her life and career. She was born in the '60s, when women in the workforce were not yet making much progress and

Sondra Samuels

the landmark legislation above had just been passed. Her formative years were ones where that choppy, uneven, but upward progress began emerging, both for women and people of color.

After earning her MBA in the late '80s and taking on roles overseas and in Ameri-Corps back home, she took on a private sector career for the next seven years. Even that role reflected and foreshadowed what Samuels was all about. She worked at a diversity consulting firm that partners with today's diverse global marketplace by creating workplaces where all employees *perform to their full potential.* There's that phrase again, as in the definition for social progress: "creating the conditions for all individuals to reach their full potential."

Samuels had more opportunities and a better education to launch her career and life than the generation that came before her. After her consulting gig, like many of these Rebuilders, she had a moment to make an important choice in life.

For the past eleven years, Samuels has been the CEO of the Northside Achievement Zone[6] (NAZ) in north Minneapolis. NAZ is in business to put itself out of business, that is, to end generational poverty and build a culture of achievement in north Minneapolis in which all low-income children of color graduate from high school college- and career-ready. This is done in partnership with thirty other nonprofits that provide wraparound supports for the entire family (housing, jobs, health, parenting education, as well as key supports through early childhood, after-school and summer programs, and K–12 school partners). No small aspiration.

Part of the reason NAZ is still very much in business is because of the way economic and social progress has slowed for African American kids in the twenty-first century. Those NAEP charts we just discussed look different over the last eleven years, when Samuels has led NAZ, as you will see in the next chapter.

"There is no NAZ without data," Samuels says, almost matter-of-factly. The data is what shows her community and key stakeholders that there is real progress, even in as complex a challenge as their mission conveys. Even more fundamentally, they use data to learn what does and doesn't work. They iterate their practices in real time to help make more progress on closing the racial achievement gap.

Sondra Samuels is an exemplar of Data Conviction. Not just because she believes in data or invests in it. Because she delivers on it. Their data is beyond inspiring.[7] NAZ students, over the course of third through eighth grade, steadily increase their proficiency in math and reading. NAZ has significantly increased students' access to early childhood education. And those NAZ scholars that enrolled in high-quality early childhood education perform much better on third-grade math and reading tests. It's a pretty compelling, clear, and data-driven improvement in the lives of more than two thousand children from nearly one thousand families.

Lots of people know data matters, and in the last five to ten years in the social sector, there are a handful of regional and national organizations that not only have better access to data, but they are *embracing* it. They make it core to who they are and how they work. It takes a leader with a deep conviction about data to get there in the first place and to sustain the investment in it.

Ultimately, where NAZ (and others playing the same serious data game Samuels is) wants to get to is sharing the data directly with the community and with parents. Then they can see what is going on in their children's and family's lives in a comprehensive way. Sondra Samuels is one of those multitalented, skilled, and experienced leaders that we are going to need to be the Rebuilders of the 2020s.

Summing Up 1950–2000

In sum, there was a wave of progress—economic, health, social—that seemed inevitably, if not always evenly, positive and shared by a majority of people over the second half of the twentieth century. But then things started to change. Really, they began changing in the '90s, but there was sort of a "frog in the frying pan" effect that hadn't turned up the heat enough yet. The sometimes-euphoric technological advances and economic growth of the '90s masked economic, social, and health fractures in America's foundation that were beginning to emerge and would widen and accelerate over the first twenty years of the new millennium.

▶   ▶   ▶

Author Note, June, 2020. There is a very important message to convey alongside the general, overall positive picture of American progress in the second half of the twentieth century. Progress was positive, on average, for the majority of Americans. But not for all Americans. Much of our progress on women's rights and racial equity, for example, has been three steps forward, then two steps back. Or sometimes three steps forward, five steps back. I don't intend to dilute the overall description here of an arc of American progress in the fifty years after World War II. It's also incorrect, perhaps immoral, to posit that perspective without also acknowledging that it was far from universal. And there are some areas, like environmental degradation, in which we regressed, for the most part, between 1950 and 2000. I say all this from my position of white male privilege.

We can't ignore the injustices of those fifty years that occurred alongside the broad progress. What we can do in 2020 is rebuild the future in ways we never could have when times were more staid and less volatile. There is an opportunity in the current upheaval of the last twenty to thirty years, particularly in the wake of COVID and the horrendous tragedy and global response to George Floyd. It's thrown many institutions and norms into a state of significant flux and has the potential to shake loose long-standing, hidebound parts of American culture and civil society that need to be rebuilt on a much stronger and very different foundation. Time will tell if all this potential can become reality. Many inequities that were unacknowledged need to be brought out into the glaring spotlight. My point of view is not about going back to the way things were in the '50s, '60s, or '70s; in fact, there are many parts of society from the latter half of the twentieth century that we need to leave behind.

I sincerely hope you will keep this personal note in mind as you read this book. I mean to paint a realistic, honest, holistic picture of our past, present, and future, one that simultaneously acknowledges America's great imperfections and its profound opportunities.

One other note. For each person I write about, I focused on them as an exemplar of a trait and made sure each story was accurate, which I verified with each of the Rebuilders. I did not ask them to agree or disagree with my broader assessment and conclusions across this entire book. I own those fully.

CHAPTER TWO

Where We Are (2000-2020)

Building hundreds of thousands of bridges across America during the second half of the twentieth century certainly helped fuel economic progress. But anything built needs to be maintained and sometimes rebuilt down the road. As we have already described, that time is now coming due for bridges.

We've all seen many of the trends and data points I get into below somewhere, sometime, in isolation. The purpose here is to pull together in one place a shared, cumulative, holistic version of what our challenges really are, including how we got here over the last twenty years. Until I took the time to look at all of these trends and this data collectively, I had seen multiple, infrequent snapshots of isolated problems in American civil society. Seeing the whole canvas sharpens the mind and clarifies the scale and scope of the challenge. And that scale and scope is what makes it so vital we have new leaders ready to take charge of all these changes going on across America.

Let's take a deeper look at the ways in which we have an America today whose progress has stalled or even reversed in the last twenty years.

Let's get this out of the way. It doesn't take a rocket scientist to know how *politically* fractured we are in America today. Politics is like the superstructure of the bridge. It matters, but the disparities in our underlying foundations (economic, health, social) are much more the root causes. Those came before the political fractures and may well be even more difficult and costly to rebuild. For the purposes of this story, politics is more of a symptom, a hot burning one, but not the underlying foundational weakness.

I'm not ignoring the political divides in America or that leadership matters there greatly. Instead, I am suggesting that many of the currents of our political divide are downstream from the economic, health, and social inequities that are more the original source of our increasingly unequal and siloed nation over the last twenty to thirty years.

Economic, 2000–2020

In the 2000s so far, the positive economic progress of most of 1950–2000 has slowed dramatically and halted or gone backward for far too many people. There was a slow, steady *decrease* in income *inequality* after World War II as the economy expanded. As we've shown, that resulted in a broadly shared, flourishing middle class for more and more Americans.

The 2000s have seen that trend line of progress go flat or downward for many people while taking a steep upward, positive arc for a smaller and smaller niche of Americans. Middle-class families (the middle 20 percent of income earners) today average $49,000 in income from sources including wages, investments, and retirement. That's $4,000 *less* than it was in 2000 (adjusted for inflation), and it includes a greater proportion of those dipping into retirement savings like pensions and 401(k)s.[1] Those data points can be a little intricate so take the time to reread them.

That is a profound change from the previous fifty years, when the income of the middle class steadily *increased*. Just to restate for emphasis: so far, in the 2000s, real income for the middle class has steadily *decreased*. We could almost say hard stop and leave it at that.

The Gini coefficient is a statistical measure intended to represent the income or wealth distribution of a nation's residents, and it is most commonly used as a measurement of income inequality. Some of the most unequal countries are South Africa, Haiti, and Botswana—probably not surprises. Some of the most equal countries, again unsurprisingly, are those in Scandinavia and, a little more surprisingly, some nations in eastern Europe.

This index of income inequality for America started increasing in the '90s and the degree of inequity has accelerated ever since. Income inequality in the United States in 2020 is closer to South Africa than it is to Sweden. The United States today ranks right between Guyana and Peru.

The point isn't that some Americans make or are worth more than others; that's to be expected in a capitalist system. The point is the *degree of inequality* and the *persistent increase* in that gap over the last thirty years. Economic *inequality* had been *declining* for decades after World War II but then started to turn in the early '90s and really accelerate in the mid-2000s, as Figure 2.1 shows.

▶ ▶ ▶

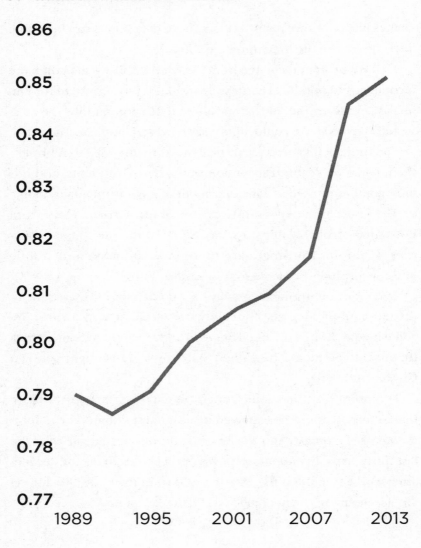

FIGURE 2.1. GINI OF NET WORTH

This ever-widening economic divide has many dimensions, including generational (see Figure 2.2). One would expect an older generation to have a higher share of wealth than younger, wealth-building generations. But nothing like the discrepancy we have today. The degree of and increase in the divergence of the wealth potential of younger generations, at similar stages of their lives, does not bode well.

Intergenerational wealth
Share of national wealth owned by each generation, by median cohort age

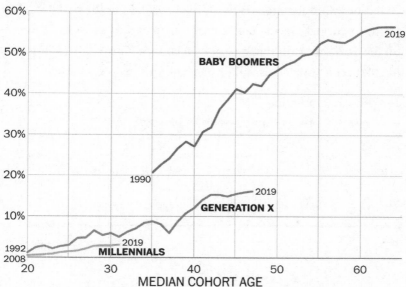

Source: Federal Reserve Distributional Accounts   THE WASHINGTON POST
Chart adapted from Gray Kimbrough

FIGURE 2.2

One more divide that is not only growing but seems to have ever-amplifying implications all across American civil society is the stark disparity in economic security in rural versus urban areas. As NPR reported just a few years ago,[2] "Rural communities still haven't recovered the jobs they lost in the [2008–9] recession. . . . [There are] shuttered coal mines on the edges of rural towns and boarded-up gas stations on rural main streets. In these [economic] data are the angers, fears, and frustrations of much of rural America. . . .

"The identity of rural communities used to be rooted in work. . . . It used to be that, when someone first arrived at these towns, they knew what people did and that they were proud to do it.

"That's not so clear anymore. How do you communicate your communal identity when the work once at the center of that identity is gone?"

That now-familiar story is definitively backed up by real data. Job growth in rural America has still not returned to pre–Great Recession levels, a sobering statistic on its own (see Figure 2.3). Obviously the 2020 economic crisis will exacerbate this even further.

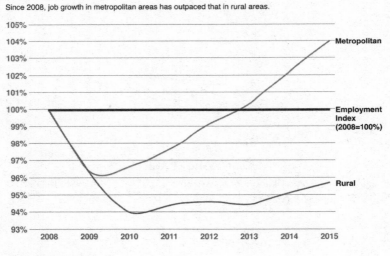

Job growth in America

Since 2008, job growth in metropolitan areas has outpaced that in rural areas.

FIGURE 2.3

Over the last twenty to thirty years, what's grown appreciably is the percentage of people at both extremes of the economic spectrum—poverty-stricken and the ultrawealthy—while the proportion in the proverbial middle class has been steadily shrinking. In sum, income inequality in the United States has hit its highest level since the Census Bureau started tracking it more than five decades ago.[3]

What Happens When You Don't Have Any More Bandwidth?

One of the Rebuilders who knows and lives and breathes the economic and health challenges of the rural-urban divide is Dreama Gentry. To be honest, I wasn't sure which trait to align Gentry with.

Dreama Gentry

Maybe that's why, sort of by default, she landed in Complexity Capacity. If we had a trait called "jack-of-all-trades," Gentry might fit that too. She is the executive director of Partners for Education (PFE)[4] at Berea College, Kentucky, about forty-five minutes down I-75, south of Lexington.

PFE's mission is to ensure all Appalachian students succeed, using four interconnected strategies—Lifting Educational Aspirations, Building Academic Skills, Connecting College and Career, and Engaging Families. That is all to optimize results for more than fifty thousand young people and their families. Just one data point: between 2013 and 2016, they increased the percentage of "kindergarten-ready students" in the Berea College Promise Neighborhood area from 16 to 36 percent.

Gentry could also show up in the 24-7 Authenticity chapter to come, because in rural areas leaders are known more personally and live in place more often. That's just the way it is. A leader has to be "24-7" because it is 24-7. Communities evaluate your authenticity based on how long term your commitment is to the place. If you and your organization take a "this is just a job until we move on" approach, you won't have the credibility to do the work. As Gentry often says, "In rural communities, it's the deep, long-term relationships that matter."

Gentry might also be an exemplar of a Generosity Mindset. PFE has learned that in such a resource-scarce area as rural Kentucky, if partners fight among themselves, they don't have a chance. The only strategy that makes sense is to grow the collective pie for everyone. While it's not always easy to have an abundance mindset in a resource poor region, PFE helps its partners understand that it's a losing proposition long term if you think scarcity. This is why she and her team spend their time working with local partners to help them align their efforts to support the educational needs of kids in their community.

The aligning of partners also suggests why Gentry fits with Cross-Sector Fluency, because so many of the projects PFE is involved in require cross-sector work. She has to work with cross-sector partners because there are relatively fewer of them. To succeed in reaching their goal, partners learn they literally cannot stay in sector silos. Gentry supports community success by creating results-oriented plans with broad community buy-in.

If you add all that up, what you have is a leader who, more than anything, has a supreme capacity for complexity. She is the closest leader, along with Trish Millines, that I think could check the boxes for all five traits. The biggest constraint on her capacity is both fascinating and frustrating. The trap is, as she explains it, that "too often people think only of roots and not of wings. People need both; they need deep roots in a community, and they need the wings to fly and see the world from a different perspective."

She loves where she lives and the people she works with. She also knows she will never be able to help all Appalachia students succeed if she doesn't think beyond Berea. That's also true of Sondra Samuels in Minneapolis; if she thinks only of north Minneapolis, her lens is too constrained. Gentry is constantly trying to get the partners in PFE to think at a regional, systemic level, not just a local, programmatic level.

Excuse my rural stereotypes here, but talking to Gentry reminds me of my aunts and uncles when I was growing up in "big city" Des Moines, Iowa. They lived in Palisades, Nebraska (having grown up in Hamlet, of course); Zeeland and Marshall, Michigan; and Anderson, Indiana. They were just a lot more no-BS kind of people.

I can think of no better person and context to learn something outside the box from than Dreama Gentry in Berea, Kentucky. Not because it's sort of cute and small and rural, but because their challenges have a different kind of complexity; one I can stand to learn a lot from. If leaders like Samuels hang around leaders like Gentry (and vice versa), their worlds get bigger and the solutions become more achievable.

Health, 2000–2020

The American health-care system in the 2000s has created a world where the health of the general population has stagnated, at best. The wealthiest have increasing access to better, more sophisticated care because they can pay for it. And lower-income, especially rural, Americans have access to lower-quality care.

The life expectancy of Americans declined for three years in a row from 2016 to 2018, an almost unfathomable statistic a generation ago. (It finally stopped and gently reversed in 2019, but barely.) In contrast to 1950–2000, average life expectancy increased by just four years from 2000 to 2020 (yes, there is some upper limit on length of life). That is an average increase of 0.2 years annually versus 0.5 in the previous fifty years. Numbers that small and precise can lose a bit of their significance, but a decrease of that magnitude in a twenty-year period has not happened since before 1900 (excepting the effects of the Spanish Flu and two world wars).

Even more vitally, to the point of this book, the disparity in health outcomes is widening. In my own community, King County, which has one of the best public health systems in America, the difference in your life expectancy, by zip code, is staggering.[5] If you start in Medina, a suburb of Bellevue, Washington, and drive nine miles across the 520

Bridge (or six miles as the crow flies) to downtown Seattle, you will see the average life expectancy drop more than twenty years.

According to the widely respected medical journal the *Lancet*, widening economic inequality in the United States has been accompanied by increasing disparities in health outcomes, one of the many interactions between the economic, health, and social inequities we face. Despite coverage expansions since 2010 due to the Affordable Care Act (ACA), which gave access to many that didn't have it at all, lower-income Americans still have far worse access to care than do wealthy Americans.[6] Meanwhile, the share of health-care resources devoted to care of the wealthy has risen. That's a pretty perverse fact, if you think about it.

Let's take the connection between economic and health inequity one step further. Over the last twenty-plus years, American companies have, in fact, spent more on their employees, but that increase in spending was completely absorbed by the costs of health care, with take-home wages stuck in a generation-long stagnancy.

Figure 2.4 pretty well tells the story. Over the last ten years (and in 2000–2010 as well), the rate of increase in workers' take-home earnings just about kept up with inflation. But the amount going to health-care premiums and deductibles has concurrently skyrocketed. Beginning in the 1990s, the cost of health care started to rise at double the rate of inflation. Total compensation spent on workers is increasing at probably the same rate it did in the '50s through the '80s. Any potential increase in take-home wages above the rate of inflation, though, has been devoured by the cost of health care.

When people talk about what stole the American dream, it's not immigration, it's mostly not technology. It is absolutely and primarily the cost of health care, yet for some reason that story seems to go largely untold. And all of that spending with very little in improved health outcomes to show for it.

Premiums and Deductibles Rise Faster Than Workers' Wages over Past Decade

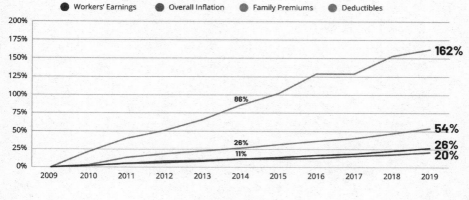

● Workers' Earnings   ● Overall Inflation   ● Family Premiums   ● Deductibles

FIGURE 2.4

The cost of health care has been the number-one cause of bankruptcy for small businesses, and it's now also the number-one cause of personal bankruptcy in America, and it's not even close. A study in the *American Journal of Public Health* in 2019 found that 66.5 percent of personal bankruptcies in the United States were due to medical issues like being unable to pay high bills or time lost from work.[7] Two-thirds of American bankruptcies. Take that statistic in for a minute.

Let's look briefly again at the rural-urban divide. Rural America is sicker, poorer, and older than the country as a whole. That puts financial pressure on the hospitals that serve it.[8] Some of this is tied to the disturbing explosion in deaths due to opioids and heroin, which both grew more than 400 percent over the first fifteen years of the twenty-first century. The vastly disproportionate number of those deaths were in lower-income and/or rural America (see Figure 2.5).[9] Just one more example of the unequal progress of American health in the twenty-first century.

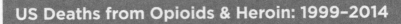

US Deaths from Opioids & Heroin: 1999–2014

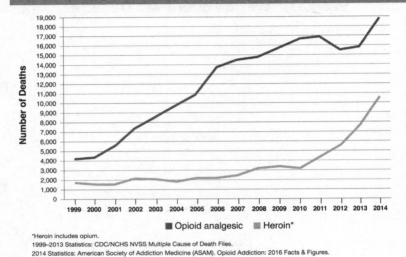

*Heroin includes opium.
1999–2013 Statistics: CDC/NCHS NVSS Multiple Cause of Death Files.
2014 Statistics: American Society of Addiction Medicine (ASAM). Opioid Addiction: 2016 Facts & Figures.

FIGURE 2.5

There are significant interconnections between all three of these forces. The growing economic divide leads to greater divides in access to quantity and quality of health care, which creates growing social disconnection. In an interview on CNN in early April 2020, Bill Gates laid bare the inequity in, for example, testing for COVID in America.[10] As he bluntly said, "If you have a relationship with the doctor that has a connection to the lab, you'll get to the front of the line. Testing is a scarce resource that is about saving lives and *allocating it in a just way.*" Health inequality and disparity has steadily grown to the highest levels in decades.

Social, 2000–2020

Unequal progress on social issues does not always reflect an unfair world. Some unequal and disparate progress is inevitable. But when those unequal opportunities have less and less to do with rewarding hard work, personal merits, or entrepreneurial risk taking, the world feels unfair to more people, it weakens social cohesion, and contributes to less trust in institutions and, ultimately, in each other.

Let's quickly revisit our definition of social progress as "the capacity of a society to . . . create the conditions for all individuals to reach their full potential." The devolution of those social conditions and the decreasing opportunities for all individuals to reach their potential has had perhaps an even deeper, more foundational effect than the increasing income and health disparities over the last twenty years.

Just as we saw with economic and health indicators, progress basically stopped once we got into the 2000s. Let's look at data on those same NAEP scales for math as well as reading (see Figure 2.6). We see the slow, but real progress (in dashed lines from 1970 to 2004) stop and completely level off (the solid lines between 2004–2020) over the last fifteen years.

The improvement over the previous thirty-five-year period has been stymied with a fifteen-year flat line. As we've said before, the fifteen-year flatline was pre-COVID; it's unavoidable that we will see further declines in academic progress in the next few years at least.

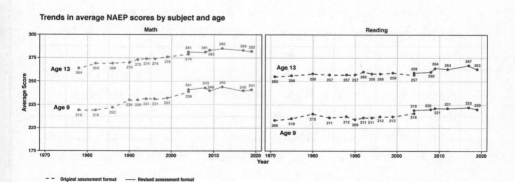

FIGURE 2.6

Given the horrendous events at a curbside in Minneapolis on May 25, 2020, the lack of social progress, as it relates to racial equity over the last twenty years, is starkly self-evident. Its ramifications will last throughout the decade ahead. All of these trends we've talked about here created, in part, the underlying conditions that led to the tragedy of George Floyd and of untold numbers of African Americans over the decades.

It is now out in the white-hot spotlight of global awareness and protest. This is a once-in-a-century opportunity for progress, and it will take every Rebuilder possible, in communities and corporations, to make that change a reality. Making true, real, systemic change on black-white relations in America could be perhaps the most significant social development of the twenty-first century.

Whether you believe its roots were in the liberal policies adopted in the 1960s or the anti-government rhetoric of the 1980s or the political discord of the 2010s, the collective belief and trust in government has plummeted, especially at the federal level. For example, between 1973 and today, confidence in small businesses and the military has remained just about even, while confidence in Congress has declined from 42 percent to 11 percent.[11] There is no other major institution in America—courts, churches, and so on—of the seventeen that Gallup has measured every year over time that is any lower; nothing is even close. Once more, assumptions that were deeply embedded coming out of World War II have been shaken, sometimes to the core, in the 2000s.

How has this all affected the attitudes of Americans? Only 37 percent believe that today's children will grow up to be better off than their parents. Americans ages eighteen to twenty-nine are more optimistic than Americans over age fifty, but nearly half of eighteen- to twenty-nine-year-olds hold the view that the next generation will be worse off. Americans ages fifty and older are particularly downbeat. Just 32 percent say their children will be better off and 61 percent think they will be worse off.[12] This is not the way it was growing up in previous generations, particularly in the second half of the 1900s.

I would be remiss if I didn't point out areas where we have, in fact, seen significant social progress in the 2000s, always on that choppy, never-straight road to progress. The #MeToo movement has made groundbreaking progress. The improvement in rights for LGBTQ Americans has also been significant, topped off by the June 2015 Supreme Court ruling for the right of same-sex couples to marry on the same terms and conditions as opposite-sex couples. Both cases would also remind us that there is a long way still to go to truly remove the totality of inequity across America on both women's and LGBTQ rights.

Economic, health, and social inequality have steadily grown to the highest levels in decades. We've seen how intertwined all of these disparities are and how they feed off of and more deeply embed each on its own and collectively. That's the very definition of a vicious cycle; it must be interrupted. It will take new leaders with a set of vital traits that have never been called upon this urgently.

Sometimes It's Just Who Someone Is

Michael Smith has lived his life and career proximate to the economic, social, and health stories we've been detailing. He grew up in the '80s and '90s, perhaps benefiting from some of the educational and social progress we described back in "Where We've Come From." He graduated and launched his professional career in the mid to late 1990s when the stagnating progress discussed in this chapter started to take hold. I have little doubt he will play a meaningful, powerful role as a Rebuilder in helping answer the question "Where are we going?"

Smith emanates generosity; it's in his personality, his spirit. I have felt and seen that in him ever since I met him more than ten years ago. I know it's in his DNA. In Smith's case, it's nature and nurture. He grew up in a low-income community. He was mindful that no one *had to* take care of one another but everyone *did.* He'd spend his summers at his neighborhood Boys & Girls Club or with his grandparents in rural North Carolina. The church was a big part of his family and early life, in which everyone took care of everyone else. He grew up surrounded by people with a Generosity Mindset.

Michael Smith

I don't want to just equate an obvious personality trait with a vital leadership trait. That's too easy and often misses the point. This is not about being nice. A Generosity Mindset is about how you approach a challenge, trying to look for the common ground, being the person that keeps the discussion open and goal-focused.

Because Michael had generosity heaped upon him, his credo in life is "To whom much is given, much will be required (Luke 12:48). That spirit took him to lead My Brother's Keeper Alliance (MBK), which aims to lead a cross-sector (there's that phrase again) national call to action focused on building safe and supportive communities for boys and young men of color.

They've selected nineteen organizations across ten states and Puerto Rico as national models to expand evidence-based initiatives to reduce youth violence, grow effective mentorship programs, and measurably improve the lives of boys and young men of color. I don't think I can overstate how vital their mission has been and how much greater it has now become.

His leadership role at MBK, Smith told me, requires him to constantly be thinking about pathways for people, about who else needs to be at the table, and always going the extra mile. At the end of our conversation, he posed an interesting question: "I still ask myself, do nice guys finish first? Or last?" He says it's his nature to turn the other cheek but wonders if he needs to be a more tough, uncompromising leader, aka more of a tough guy. (I'll refer him to the stories on 24-7 Authenticity to answer that one.)

I'm not sure about nice guys, but I've seen it time and time again when a truly authentic Generosity Mindset can change the room. I've seen a roomful of geniuses with hundreds of years of collective experience fall flat on their faces because everyone was playing a zero-sum game. The value, the raw positive power, of a Generosity Mindset is profound. Michael Smith doesn't need to become a tough guy.

Summing Up 2000-2020

America's bridges need to be rebuilt. Is it more complex to build something new from raw materials or rebuild it when it is in a state of disrepair? Was it a bigger challenge to build America's system of more than 600,000 bridges, beginning with the Frankford Avenue Bridge in northeast Philadelphia in 1697, than it will be to rebuild and repair the 47,000–235,000 bridges that are in varying states of structural deficiency today? We know that rebuilding will require something different—a different mindset, different skills, and a different, sustained intent.

Metaphorically, Rebuilders are leaders that are great at coming to a big table with a whole bunch of Legos spread all over the place. They are world class at how you rearrange and redistribute the Lego pieces to optimize the configuration. In the decade ahead, we are going to be working much more with the Legos we currently have than with a whole bunch of new Legos we wish we had. Rebuilders know how to rearrange and optimize the pieces we have, knowing they are not going to get new pieces for a while.

Rebuilders, like the ones you're reading about, haven't been as elevated in our leadership zeitgeist over the past twenty years as much as all of the innovators. Our leaders in the years ahead can't just be builders, they have to be Rebuilders. That's what our unequal, siloed world calls us to be. As has always been and always will be the case when the challenges ahead are daunting, these times call for a new kind of leader.

CHAPTER THREE

Amplifiers

n the Introduction, we noted that most bridges stand for a long time, in part by carefully balancing two forces, compression and tension. Bridges don't fail very often, but when they do, they always collapse for the same reason: something happens that makes them unable to balance those two forces.[1]

One force becomes too great, too amplified, for one of the bridge components (maybe something as simple as a single rivet or tie-bar), which then fails. That means the amplified load suddenly has to be shared by fewer components. Sooner or later, another component fails, then another, and so the bridge collapses in a kind of domino effect.

At the same time as economic, social, and health progress are becoming more disparate and unequal, we have these incredible amplifiers—technology and media—that are accelerating these destabilizing trends even more. They make it easier to create a negative domino effect, analogous to the one that causes bridges to collapse, instead of keeping our country connected and strong, like the parts of a sturdy bridge.

Economic, social, and health inequities will always happen throughout history, but *not* at the stunning rates so far in the 2000s, especially the 2010s. The foundations of American civil society—economic, social, health—are as shaky these days as many of our bridges across America. Technology, media, and now COVID, are amplifying those fractures at an alarming rate. This is a complex set of accelerating changes that needs leaders that can take charge for the good of America's economic, social, and health future.

Amplifier Number One: Tech

Technology amplifies inequality and inequity. A useful construct from the 2019 Human Development Review[2] helps us understand the effects of amplifiers. The report defines human progress in terms of "basic" and "enhanced" capabilities and living standards. Basic capabilities are those elements of life that are about getting out of poverty, like mortality rates, access to basic needs and wants in life, and so on. Sort of equivalent to the basic levels in Maslow's hierarchy of needs. Most will agree that we saw progress for most people from 1950 to 2000 in basic economic, health, and social living standards.

Enhanced capabilities are those aspects of life that become more important in a twenty-first-century society, things like advanced education and access to more sophisticated technologies; things that were once considered almost luxuries have become critical to living and thriving in a knowledge economy. People who are empowered today with enhanced capacities will be even further ahead tomorrow and create greater social inequality; that is part of the "Where We Are" story of the last twenty years.

Access to technology at a basic level is *converging* and more universally available, but at a more enhanced level it's *diverging*. Here's an example: most Americans, at home or via the public library or somewhere, have access to the internet and some basic form of computing. But the percentage of American adults that have the "full suite" of enhanced tech tools (a smartphone, a laptop, broadband, and a tablet) ranges from 18 percent for people with an annual income of $30,000 to 64 percent for those with an income of more than $100,000.[3] Having access to that full suite, and the skills and capacities and money to use them, is what creates great opportunity for some but not for others.

Here's another example, rural versus urban, of just one of those enhanced tech tools: access to high-speed internet (see Figure 3.1). The same discrepancy would be true if we looked at just about any other tech tool, and its effects were starkly amplified in the spring and fall of 2020 in schools all across America.

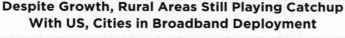

Despite Growth, Rural Areas Still Playing Catchup With US, Cities in Broadband Deployment

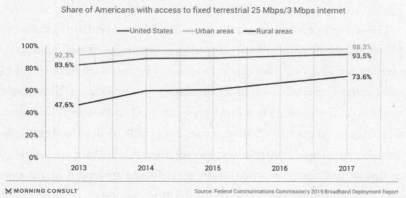

FIGURE 3.1

Inherently and increasingly, technology leads to more jobs on the high end of the skill spectrum and fewer in the middle.[4] What seemed so widely positive and optimistic about technology in the '90s leaves us with looming questions today:

► Can the widening gap between basic and enhanced capabilities in technology be narrowed, or will it continue to widen and accentuate tech as an amplifier of inequity?

► Will we ultimately be more or less connected as human beings because of technology?

► Is machine learning going to be more helpful or harmful to people? (Machine learning is the ability of computer systems to automatically learn without being programmed.)

► How do we create consistently secure online experiences in which I know I'm not the victim of bots or going to be hacked?

► Will the creators and deployers of artificial intelligence use it for better or worse in the world around us? (Artificial intelligence is a computer system's ability to perform tasks that normally require human intelligence, such as speech recognition and decision-making.)

These are not hypothetical questions; they are real and profound questions about whether the amplifier of technology will lead us to a better world . . . or not. The jury is out. The message here is not to paint some Luddite vision of technology as being all bad; that would be absurd. Technology has huge positives and has created innumerable enhancements to quality of life, especially in developing countries. For example, mobile technology is contributing to financial inclusion in countries without an established financial infrastructure, and global markets create trade opportunities.[5]

If we look at the rates of adoption of new technologies and innovations across American society, it's clear that adoption happens much more quickly today than it did in the 1900s (see Figure 3.2). In general, that's a good thing for civil society.

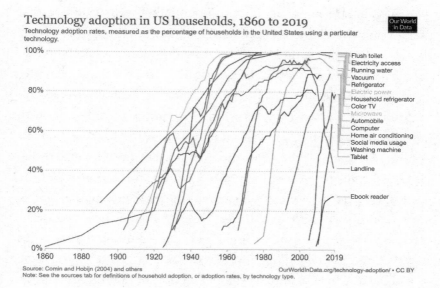

Technology adoption in US households, 1860 to 2019

Technology adoption rates, measured as the percentage of households in the United States using a particular technology.

FIGURE 3.2

Our challenge is not whether technology has done the world any good. It has. The question is whether the value the average American will accrue from it in the future is going to be increasingly *convergent* or *divergent*. It's a vital question with huge implications for leaders. The answer will determine whether technology returns to being more of an amplifier for good than for inequality or worse.

Amplifier Number Two: Media

Media is a fast-expanding amplifier of silos and separation. This is a fact regardless of where you are on any political or economic spectrum. In less than one generation, we went from three mainstream networks giving a fairly balanced, somewhat homogenized (admittedly with a left-wing bent) version of the news, to an incredibly dispersed media system of hyper-customization. You can completely customize your intake of all media sources to just fit "your tribe."[6]

We all can, and many people do, essentially live in a bubble that serves only to validate what we want to hear.

This means accepting "bias" in news and having a much greater ability to bypass news altogether. Ideas like "an informed electorate" and "responsible citizenship" can be rendered meaningless, except to your tribe. I was driving across the I-90 bridge the other day with my nineteen-year-old, and I asked him what he was looking at on his phone. He said Reddit. Over the next few minutes, I learned that it's, by far, his primary source of news and information about the world. He's not an outlier. You can look at this data on either side of the political aisle, and it's extreme. Figure 3.3 shows how Democrats look at various news sources. It just takes a few minutes to look at the sources one by one and digest the message.

Media also acts to amplify the perception of unevenness and inequality, To state the obvious, media and tech create a reinforcing cycle, a spin cycle that spins faster and faster. If you find this a little unnerving, join me. This dynamic is going to be hard to unwind or slow down, and it will be hard to get us back to at least some sense of shared news and information.

We haven't even started on *social* media. Everything we'd say about media in general applies ten times, if not more. Social media has never been regulated or managed like other forms of media. That is a challenge by itself. Traditional media needs to compete with one hand tied behind its back because it has some rules it has to follow.

On social media, you instantly get biased, rushed reporting that has lost most editorial control (because social media has essentially no rules). Things are spinning faster and faster and it's hard to know how to unwind. That's a subject for another book, but in this context, just know social media is making our megachallenges even more challenging and the disparities ever greater.

Just like tech, let's acknowledge that the spread of media sources has positives. There is more transparency, people are far more

Democrats' trust and distrust of news sources

% of Democrats and Democratic leaners who trust or distrust each source for political and election news

Sources that are <u>trusted</u> by more Democrats than distrusted

	Distrust	Trust	% who have heard of each
NPR	2%	46%	59%
PBS	4	56	84
BBC	5	48	76
NBC News	6	61	93
CBS News	6	59	91
ABC News	7	60	93
New York Times	6	53	84
Time	6	46	84
Washington Post	7	47	80
CNN	10	67	95
Newsweek	5	31	74
Politico	3	21	49
MSNBC	9	48	86
Wall Street Journal	7	38	79
USA Today	8	35	85
Univision	3	13	51
The Guardian	6	17	55
Business Insider	4	11	48
The Hill	4	11	34
Vox	6	10	40
Huff Post	14	20	66
Vice	10	12	44

Sources that are <u>distrusted</u> by more Democrats than trusted

	Distrust	Trust	% who have heard of each
New York Post	20	13	69
BuzzFeed	21	10	68
Washington Examiner	9	4	33
Fox News	61	23	92
Daily Caller	9	<1	15
Breitbart	36	1	42
Limbaugh (radio)	43	1	50
Hannity (radio)	38	<1	44

FIGURE 3.3

informed, and people can't hide facts (though they can distort them). Perpetrators like Harvey Weinstein and Jeffrey Epstein are revealed in the hot spotlight of public exposure. Our struggle, of course, is rediscovering some common shared facts and truths, and a wide swath of actors are fighting against us.

Does It Matter in the Huddle?

If anyone knows how to be an amplifier of social media, it's a celebrity, a famous athlete. The interview with the athlete is often one of

the pinnacles of inane, meaningless, banal commentary, basically the opposite of authenticity. You occasionally get the athlete considered brash (Diana Taurasi), funny (Charles Barkley), or offbeat (Phil Mickelson), but *authentic* and *pro athlete* rarely find themselves in the same sentence. Doug Baldwin is the rare pro athlete that personifies what 24-7 Authenticity is all about.

Doug Baldwin

It doesn't get much more "authentic" than running a crossing route in an NFL game, waiting to catch a pass. Eleven opponents are ready to hit you very hard within a millisecond of catching that pass. That's what Doug Baldwin did for eight seasons, hundreds of times each season, playing for the Seattle Seahawks. What does football have to do with the future of leadership? In Baldwin's case, a lot.

For all the exemplars of authenticity I studied and talked to, everyone's path was a little different. Baldwin's upbringing was solid, but his family didn't talk much about feelings, which sounds familiar to me about my family growing up. Over the course of five years, Baldwin made the big transitions from south Florida to Stanford and then to the NFL. The white-hot media spotlight of the NFL clarified and sharpened things for him. It's a stage that enabled him to watch and observe, start to understand his own feelings, and "see a lot of different ways to be a man."

In Baldwin's case, the metaphorical "playing field" for his work is literal. I wondered how something like authenticity, or lack of, plays out in a game with your team on the field. Is that even a relevant dynamic to winning or losing? He said it shows up in the huddle just as it would in a corporate meeting.

In those moments when it really matters, in the last drive in a tie game in the fourth quarter, if you don't have authentic relationships, someone won't always go the extra mile for a teammate. The same goes for an important community meeting, where there is no game clock, but there is just as much urgency. It's as basic as this—if you are not authentic, you cannot build genuine, lasting relationships. And without those relationships, you can't win. You will lose because you need the team.

Few of us have as clear of a scoreboard as an NFL athlete. Baldwin's next scoreboard is to build the Family First Community Center in Renton, Washington, which will reach hundreds of families and thousands of youth in the community where he and Richard Sherman first landed when he moved to Seattle.

Doug Baldwin is a person that wants you to see him for who he is. As long as you understand him authentically, he's okay if you do or don't like him. We are going to need leaders from all over American civil society in the decade ahead from unusual places like sports. I don't just mean team captain or the leader of a team on the field of play.

More athletes have begun to speak out on subjects outside of sports in the last few years and, whether you agree with them or not, their views and perspectives matter and are heard. The broad impact they had in the spring and summer of 2020 was profound, and not just in sports but in voting rights, police reform, and so on. For athletes to have their voices heard, and for them to be leaders, is going to take them having the highest level of accountability for authenticity. Baldwin is a person that meets that bar.

We haven't heard the last of Baldwin, just because he retired a year ago. He has been very focused on the issues that have been pressing on our nation for too long now. At a 2016 press conference responding to the deaths of Keith Lamont Scott and Terrence Crutcher, he said, "When you see numerous instances like this happen again and again . . . you're asking questions. . . . We understand that there's an inherent risk that comes with being a police officer. But that should not be the case of being a citizen in the United States. There should not be an inherent risk when you have an encounter with law enforcement. . . . I think that we're raising a culture in society right now that is questioning that very sentiment. . . . It's not OK."[7] Baldwin, the son of a police offer, unfortunately continues to be correct.

And the Ultimate Amplifier in 2020: COVID

It almost goes without saying that COVID is further amplifying all of this. COVID (1) accelerates tech and media as amplifiers, (2) accentuates the economic, health, and social disparities, and (3) is its own form of amplifying inequity unto itself. A triple effect.

Axios put it this way: "The virus itself doesn't discriminate but it does reflect the racial and socioeconomic disparities of the cities where it's spreading and the health care system that struggled to contain it. Many of the people who are disproportionately hurt by the virus have the least control over or say in the system. The pandemic is exposing and deepening many of the nation's great divides."[8] Metaphorically, there are disparities across civil society being pushed in through the throat end of a megaphone and coming out the mouth end, having been increasingly amplified as they travel along the neck. And the volume and diameter of the whole megaphone just keeps increasing.

From a straightforward health standpoint, not only does poverty create conditions ripe for the spread of a respiratory pathogen, but the conditions of COVID also create an economy ripe for the spread of poverty. This will likely become another vicious (not virtuous) cycle of an amplifier. Low-income populations will see case surges, and case surges will push those populations deeper into poverty. And it will keep going into 2021 and who knows how long into the decade ahead.

CHAPTER FOUR

Where Are We Going?

t's very clear that we live in an increasingly unequal and siloed America over the last twenty years. Yes, it was always that way to some degree, in a capitalist economy, but nothing even close to the intensity and acceleration since 2000. It's not just a political divide or some fabrication of MSNBC or Fox News. Parts of our American civic foundation "are structurally deficient and in need of urgent repairs," just like America's bridges. That set of diverging conditions for America is critical context for leaders in the future.

To rebuild, we need to leverage the strengths of the American society today (not those of seventy or even twenty years ago), namely the diversity of people, approaches, perspectives, and backgrounds. That diversity of people, place, and power is what will lead us to better and stronger leaders that will make rebuilding possible at all. Diversity aimed at a shared purpose, not merely diversity for diversity's sake. Diversity empowered with a common goal and shared interest.

To be very clear, this is my one explicit political paragraph: this is about going forward to a new future, not a return to some "glorious past" with any MAGA-type inferences. We need to rebuild, but not return to, many of the systemic weaknesses that got us here in the first place. The entire "Where We Are" chapter points out many ways in which we are paying for not paying enough attention to the increasingly unequal outcomes across America.

Our leadership hasn't caught up with many of these changes. The pace of change the last ten to twenty years is dizzying, and taking charge of it gets more unclear by the day. The equation to solve is now far more complex, multivariate, and will require new kinds and updated versions of skill sets and qualities. We will find leaders for our future in less expected places, in neighborhoods, community organizations, sports teams, and so on in addition to corporate America. Some individual leaders are more ready than others. You're reading about them. But leadership as a fundamental asset in our civil society—across our private, public, and social sectors—has not yet adapted nearly *enough*.

A Master's in Cross-Sector Fluency

This book is centered on America. David Risher is American, but he is the one leader in this book whose primary domain is interna-

David Risher

tional. I made that exception because he is one of the most cross-sector fluent leaders I've ever known.

Across the twentieth century, America progressed from 90 percent literacy to more than 99 percent. Globally, that data point went from 20 percent to 85 percent, which means about one billion people are still illiterate. David Risher is working on that last 15 percent, and he is a quintessential example of a leader with native, exceptional Cross-Sector Fluency.

He spent twenty-plus years in high tech and then decided, based on a lightning bolt moment on a family vacation, to create a non-profit, Worldreader. Over the years of doing work on literacy in Africa, he learned the hard, important lesson that he cannot solve the systemic problem without the government, the public sector. Up to that point, he'd run a nonprofit that knew how to leverage the private sector. But ultimately, it took Risher's growing experiences across all three sectors to make Worldreader what it is today: in seven countries, more than 500 schools, and with 15,735,473 new readers since 2010 (as of October 20, 2020). That kind of facility across all three sectors is a hallmark of the new kind of leader our world needs and demands as we move into the 2020s.

For Risher, let's look at it in both directions, both from and to the private and nonprofit sector. There are some fundamental, vital lessons about being a Rebuilder. I'm going to boil it down to what I think the single most important lesson was for Risher, from both directions in his career.

Let's start with what he learned during his for-profit days at Microsoft and Amazon that apply to the nonprofit and public sector work he has been doing the last ten years (and probably the next ten). In the private sector, you start with the customer and work back to the products and services needed. In the social sector, it's often the other way around: someone has an idea or program, they try and see if it works, people might get fired up about having what appears to be some positive change, and then they go from there. Maybe that is effective in some situations, but too often it turns out to be unsustainable.

Risher asked himself what illiterate people in the word need and what products and services would best meet their needs. Just as he would have clarified what a user of software needs and build a product to meet those needs. That customer-first orientation has been vital to Risher at Worldreader.

Worldreader had a good start, raised some money, made some noise, got some great press, and shipped good products. But they weren't making the progress they needed to make several years in. At that point, Risher and his team did a full pivot and looked first at what their "customer," illiterate people in third-world countries, needed. Since then, they have accelerated their growth and impact.

Now, let's go in the other direction: What has Risher learned at Worldreader that he would take back to the private sector? To an entrepreneur, this may seem pretty basic. When he was at Microsoft and Amazon, he had to think about product strategy and competition and driving revenues and so on. Those are individual parts of a whole core business model, which Risher never had to think about until he got to Worldreader. Here's a working definition of a business model: a design for the successful operation of a business, identifying revenue sources, customer base, products, and details of financing. A core model, though evolving and responsive to the market and customers, was already in place when he got to Microsoft and Amazon.

All that sounds a little dry but it's core to succeeding or failing by truly grasping the business model for the whole enterprise. When Risher told me that, it quickly reminded me of many private sector volunteers I worked with when I was at Social Venture Partners. A lot of them talked about how much more they learned in a few months at a scrappy, grassroots, living-month-to-month nonprofit than they did back at their day job at BigCorp. And yet, for the most part, we assume, as Risher did for a while, that the knowledge flows in just one direction. It took him several years to get clear about the new business model he had been building, and it has made a huge difference in their reach and impact today.

That assumption about the direction of knowledge might have been at least harmless (or arrogant and harmless) twenty, thirty, or fifty years ago. But now that faulty assumption is damaging at best. Companies that don't get that lesson, to look to and learn from the social sector, are not just missing big opportunities, they are putting their corporation at risk long term. Organizations with truly fluent cross-sector leaders like David Risher will not miss those opportunities or be blindsided by those risks.

P.S. When you get to know some of these Rebuilders as well as I do, sometimes you want to know a little more about what makes them tick. I've always heard Risher talk a lot about his mom, not quite as much about his dad. I asked him one day and he explained, "My dad's standards were crazy high for himself, and that probably rubbed off on me. It had a lot to do with being one of the only black partners in a DC law firm.[1] He felt a huge pressure to succeed, not just for himself, but for African Americans in DC." That alone tells us more about David Risher and why he's a great leader today.

He went on to say, "We'd watch boxing on TV, go to Bullets games at the Cap Center, read together, particularly on the one vacation he allowed himself each year. One year we graded LSATs together at the beach. Watching him do the Sunday *New York Times* crossword in pen—something I do to this day, and think about him every Sunday."

David Risher is a Sunday-*New-York-Times*-crossword-puzzle-in-pen kind of person. Trish Millines is a what-you-see-is-what-you-get leader. Rosanne Haggerty is a steely-eyed-and-Generosity-Mindset leader. The three of them and Felipe Moreno, Doug Baldwin, Sondra Samuels, Dreama Gentry, Michael Smith, Dan Cardinali, and the other twenty-nine rebuilders you'll read about are what give me hope.

More than hope. They are our bridges to the future. We can rebuild the foundations of America, both our bridges, and our civil society. Read on, learn from, and be inspired and guided by their stories of taking charge of change for a better America.

PART THREE

The Five Vital Traits

There isn't a new noun or verb I'm anchoring to here that hasn't been written about as a leadership trait somewhere at some time. That's not the point about Rebuilders. Look at and think about all five vital traits, as parts of a connected whole, not just individually. We will amplify these five interconnecting traits by telling the stories of exemplars of those traits and of leaders already in place, and taking charge of change, in communities and companies across America.

They are leaders who don't necessarily have a classic organization role as a CEO or executive director. They are at the top of organizations, in the middle of departments, or on the street in a neighborhood. We need leaders at lots of levels in lots of places. One of the exemplars, Richard Woo, talks about "organization-less leaders." That's a useful frame for many Rebuilders.

We will look at each of the traits, one at a time, through the experiences and excellence of a handful of exemplars of each. We'll provide a definition of each trait, look at downsides of each, and some takeaways. I hope you will read the rest of these stories not just for inspiration but for how you can take action. I hope the corners and edges of the pages (if you don't use an e-reader or audiobook) will get worn and torn in a few places.

Seventy-five percent of the stories are about leaders in the nonprofit or public sector. Ten of the thirty-eight Rebuilders had significant or primary or only experience in the private sector, so it's well accounted for. But we are very accustomed to seeing private sector leaders called out as the exemplars of leadership. Part of bringing the focus to a new path of leadership is showing you leaders that don't always end up in the classic management or leadership books or stories.

 THE FOUNDATIONS OF American civil society, like tens of thousands of bridges across America, are deteriorating. There are many connected parts of the foundation, substructure, and superstructure of a bridge that need to be looked at holistically before a plan is developed to rebuild. We need to look at these leaders holistically, and the five vital, connected traits, to rebuild our communities and companies across America.

A Little about Me

Over the last thirty-five years, I've transitioned from a fourteen-year private sector career to sixteen years in the nonprofit sector and now to a consulting practice over the last five years. That journey has brought me in contact with all three sectors, including the public sector in multiple, extensive assignments in my consulting work. It's given me firsthand experiences with and a wide-angle perspective on the increasingly hyperamplified, unequal and siloed America that is the setting for this book.

I'm not some unicorn, but I've accrued the benefit of a range and depth of experiences across all three sectors, including:

- ▶ Working inside two global corporations, in very different industries, including the hypergrowth days at Microsoft in the 1990s. I held marketing, operations, and general management roles with significant profit-and-loss responsibility.

- ▶ Being part of a start-up that failed, where we fell on our faces and learned a lot that I repeatedly applied later in life.

- ▶ Being the founding president of a global network of thousands of civic and philanthropic leaders in forty-plus cities in eight countries, the largest of its kind in the world.

- ▶ Acting as a coach and mentor to small-business owners for several years, working through a myriad of their people, strategic, and financial challenges.

- ▶ Working alongside and sometimes mentoring nonprofit leaders who were leading small and large as well as local, regional, and national organizations

- ▶ Being a full-time consultant on projects that aimed to create national- and local-level change across all three sectors and aspired to address a wide range of social issues, including poverty, arts, and health care.

- ▶ Building a personal network of business and social sector leaders that has been my number-one professional asset for more than twenty years.

I'm not a particularly good innovator, but I'm a good enough renovator. I'm not very effective at assembling a brand-new structure, but I could do the job of reconfiguring and resizing the parts of an existing structure. If I were an engineer, I wouldn't be the one to design something like new Lucky Knot Bridge,[1] four bridges in one, in Changsha, China, but I would be a good collaborator to begin rebuilding the tens of thousands of bridges in need of urgent repair across America.

CHAPTER FIVE

24-7 Authenticity

There are, as we've discussed, significant, growing differences in the use of and access to technology. Media today creates hyper attention and analysis. Because both act as huge amplifiers (megachallenge #1), the value and importance of 24-7 Authenticity grows by the day.

No matter what your politics, we all have skepticism about some news or information from some sources. What grows in value is genuine authenticity. It is very hard to build, very easy to lose if you misstep, and utterly invaluable, personally as well as professionally, if you can manifest it every day.

Of the five traits, 24-7 Authenticity may be the hardest one to obtain and sustain. It's a very high bar. That just speaks to the world we live in. These leaders here derived their authenticity from different places. They are living it in different ways. But every single one of them is profoundly, truly authentic. We will tell their stories not only to learn from how they show up in the world but to deconstruct some of the keys to the 24-7 platform they've reached.

Remember, 24-7 Authenticity in leaders is often paired with a strong conviction about data, which backs up and strengthens the trust built by being authentic. Data can sort of "seal the deal" and reinforce genuineness and authenticity.

> THE DECK, THE PAVEMENT, of a bridge is the tangible platform of the whole structure. It's what people can see and trust they can drive across, knowing it will be solid and enduring. Rebuilders are leaders that we can trust and that will be solid and enduring. When we think about rebuilding America, 24-7 Authenticity is a visible, tangible platform for a Rebuilder as leader.

If you think dealing with issues like authenticity . . . are not worthwhile because there are more pressing issues, like the bottom line or attendance or standardized test scores, you are sadly, sadly mistaken. It underpins everything. —BRENÉ BROWN

From a "Rising Star" to an "Angry Black Man"

Michael McAfee didn't grow up in poverty in Oakland, California, but his family often didn't have much more than what they needed. Though there was a shortage of economic assets early in his life, his parents—a chauffeur (dad) and nurse's aide (mom)—always made sure the family was safe and had what they needed.

McAfee gained one of his first leadership lessons by watching his parents. Their careers were about helping people in one way or another. He credits that modeling to this day, saying their example has "never left my psyche." As he was growing up, his parents gave him the opportunity to attend a high school across town to give him a different perspective on the world. He never lost track of his roots, but in a new environment, he began to see what else was possible.

Michael McAfee

There are many different journeys to 24-7 Authenticity; that's how McAfee's started out. In his twenties, he began to figure out there was a bigger table of wealth and power—one for him to understand and learn about, to someday get burned by, but ultimately have a full seat at in order to influence wealth and power for social change. Many Rebuilders have critical decision points, but perhaps no one has had more forks in the road, and invaluable mentors in life, than McAfee. Fork in the road number one came in his junior year of college. One day while studying at the University of Central Missouri, he woke up and learned that his girlfriend was pregnant. A baby girl was on the way and he was going to be a father. He was completely at a loss and in a panic about ruining his life. He walked to the office of one of his mentors at the time, ROTC Captain John Garza. McAfee was looking for what he was sure would be abundant understanding and support.

He got one sentence from Garza: "You've got until 3:00 p.m. today to figure it out." Garza, in effect, said, "Get authentic, McAfee." So, he did. To this day, McAfee has a strong relationship with his daughter and her mom.

Coming out of college, McAfee was a "rising star." Within a few years, he was presented with a great professional opportunity. Another mentor saw the potential in him and he soon found himself working at one of the nation's premier community foundations. After a few years, they loaned him out to help turn around a large and struggling youth development organization. He was on an upward career trajectory. It was just the kind of challenge that a twenty-five-year-old loves to take on.

In the course of this career step, he was reacquainted with the inequities that he was familiar with from his youth. To this day, he never lost track of his roots, but now he was viewing things from a position of leadership—a whole different lens and platform than a young boy growing up in Oakland. Which brought him to fork in the road number two.

In time, McAfee approached his bosses and said, "Look, here's what I see, here's what's wrong and broken, and this is what needs to change." That wasn't the message they wanted to hear from their rising star. As McAfee tells it, he could have easily remained the star by staying quiet and saying things would just get better. He championed the issues and inequities he saw and pressed for change. By doing so, he went from being the "rising star" to an "angry black man" who was sent to anger management classes. That experience, in effect, showed him the sometimes-real cost of being authentic. 24-7 Authenticity is *not* free.

McAfee moved to Chicago and spent the next several years at the US Department of Housing and Urban Development. You know where this story goes next: fork in the road number three. After several years, another of his valued mentors in life challenged him about where he was taking his career. He could have stayed in his role at HUD and been "comfortable" (Michael's word), but he chose to move on to the next challenge. Part of being authentic is not running in place when that is the easier thing to do.

Michael McAfee became the inaugural director of the Promise Neighborhoods Institute in 2011 and today is the CEO of Policy Link.[1] He would not have gotten to this place without making the authentic decisions he did at the forks in the road in his life. More than fifty communities across America are planning or implementing results-focused, data-driven Promise Neighborhoods, scaling up to serve two hundred thousand children nationwide, representing more than seven hundred schools across the country.

There is plenty to learn from McAfee's journey. Perhaps most important is that the challenges and standards for 24-7 Authenticity are big and high. How does someone like McAfee repeatedly hold himself to those high standards? Not only do you have to reach that high standard, but you have to stay there as a leader. It's a steep climb, not an easy peak to stay upon, and there are plenty of people ready to push you off. I asked him how he holds himself account- able. His internal checklist is powerful and simple:

- ▶ Does being truly authentic bring me joy? There has to be internal reward because authenticity also comes with real risks and sometimes high costs.
- ▶ Who are you accountable to and what ultimately are you working for? Not the people you know, not the people with the big money, but the citizens that you *don't* know who are out in the communities you serve every day.
- ▶ It matters to be around money and power. Always try to influence it for the good, but never let it own you.

The last note I'll make about him is very much a manifestation of a leader with 24-7 Authenticity. He is one of those people, as is Millines, Baldwin, and others, who is as equally and authentically comfortable in the boardroom as he is on the street. He reminds me a bit of Sudha Nandagopal, whom you'll read about later. These Rebuilders are people who have a flexibility in where and how they show up. Those are significant assets for the challenges we face right now and will be facing in the decade ahead.

A Definition of 24-7 Authenticity

There's been quite a bit written about authenticity and transparency as leadership qualities. "Radical transparency"[2] has certainly been in the lexicon for ten or more years as a term to describe leaders significantly increasing the openness of organizational processes and data.

Authenticity, in the dictionary, conveys that someone is worthy of belief, is not false or an imitation, and is true to one's own personality, spirit, or character. Sometimes the dictionary definition is an awkward fit; in this case, it's very well put.

Authenticity sort of sits at the intersection of radical transparency and media-as-an-amplifier. You *need* to be authentic and open before you *have* to be. It's not as if it's optional or variable in today's world. A leader just needs to start from that as a grounding principle. And 24-7 implies a proactive quality. Not just responsively authentic, but leaning in, pushing your comfort zone on authenticity.

As with all of these attributes, it needs to become second nature. In our world of sometimes-hard-to-discern (or fake?) news, this can't be a transitory, transactional trait; it has to become a part of the essential DNA of Rebuilders for the future.

Surrendering to the Intention

When you hang around a lot of socially conscious, civically active leaders as I have the last twenty-plus years, people start to remind you of someone else you've met before, maybe a long time ago. In *Can't Not Do*, one of the people I told the story of was a social change agent named Dwight Frindt. He has a wonderful expression: "surrendering to the intention that is wanting to use your life." That could certainly apply to Reverend Debbie Little and her street ministry.

Little didn't come to her work out of some unhappiness with her life, but as a calling. It wasn't necessary to take her ministry (she is an ordained priest in the Episcopal Church) out to the streets to be authentic. But if that's where your conscience is leading you, then it's certainly authentic to follow.

I'm not suggesting every, or even most, people's journey to 24-7 Authenticity has to come through a spiritual belief. But for some it

Debbie Little

does. After thirty years happily in communications and publications work, fearful of losing salary and identity but tired of skirting around what felt to be impossible for her to do, one day she said yes.

For several years she had in her heart the desire "to learn to be a servant, to get closer to people who have nothing and learn from them how to love my neighbor." Her yes opened the door to a sequence of steps leading to seminary and ordination in order to take, as she says, "the gifts of church—community, prayer, steady presence—out to people who cannot come indoors to receive them."

She is the founder of Common Cathedral (Ecclesia Ministries). It's an outdoor congregation for people experiencing homelessness, housed and unhoused, sharing God's love through community and worship on Boston Common. Little's story is one of listening to your soul and letting it finally take you where it authentically wants to go, surrendering to the intention wanting to use her life.

I think the lesson from Debbie for some, not all, of us is to listen to that inner message and at least walk down the less expected path one day. It may not lead where you expect it to, but the willingness to explore that journey brings you closer to your own authenticity.

Something she said reminded me of Dreama Gentry in Berea, Kentucky. I asked Little how people living on the street know if you are authentic. They told her, "We never thought you'd stay out here, and you came back, and then came back again"—much as Gentry's neighbors judge the authenticity of folks, in part, by how long they are going to stick around.

How does it work, being real on the street? "They taught me," she said. "I always asked, 'Tell me about yourself; tell me about God.'

And what they told me grounded what is homeless in *me*, and brought me home."

I found Little through Rosanne Haggerty. That's the way this works sometimes. Rebuilders seem to find other Rebuilders. I was curious how something like Little's street program can be part of a holistic strategy like the ones Haggerty invests her time in. Haggerty is trying to work on whole-community, population-level change, and Little, it would seem, is "just" working a street program.

According to Haggerty, "Debbie, in her quiet way, has disrupted the faith community's response to homelessness, making it more of a relationship-based approach, not a program/charity approach, at scale. It's a network organized around common principles. We are always on the lookout for people who can execute a change vision at scale. I'm personally fascinated with the untapped potential of the faith community and how we might activate system-change thinking and action there."

As happened often when I talked to Rebuilders, there is a lot more one could unpack about that last thought alone. For now, Little is living the intention that is wanting to use her life, and Haggerty can see it as clearly as anyone.

Authenticity in an Amplified World

I've already spent time on amplifiers, but I want to emphasize one key point. Being and leading with 24-7 Authenticity in the world of technology, especially social media, has gotten logarithmically more challenging and, hence, that much more valuable.

The *Atlantic* posted an interesting scenario in a recent piece: "The Founding Fathers strove to create institutions and procedures that would work with human nature to resist the forces that had torn apart so many other attempts at self-governance. . . . But what would happen to American democracy if, one day in the early 21st century, a technology appeared that—over the course of a decade—changed several fundamental parameters of social and political life? What if this technology greatly increased the amount of 'mutual animosity' and the speed at which outrage spread?"[3]

Match that up with Georgetown University associate professor of management Christine Porath, whose research says, "Our internal thoughts don't have nearly as much power as our external language. When we say something out loud, it has ten times more power than it does when we think it. And negativity is a multiple of four to seven times more powerful than positivity. So, if I say something out loud and it's negative, it impacts me forty to seventy times more power-fully." That math is staggering.

Combine the *Atlantic* reference with Porath's research. Even if Po-rath is off by a factor of ten, the negativity that social media dissemi-nates is very powerful. That's the context and the constant battle. A leader with 24-7 Authenticity can't depend only on positive informa-tion. Rampant, self-reinforcing negativity makes the job of establishing true, deep authenticity so much harder in 2020 than it was in 2010.

A Different Lens

A lot of the 24-7 Authenticity leaders I talk to come at it from a prac-tical, lived experience, like McAfee. Andy Lipkis certainly does, too, in part, but his authenticity has a more spiritual, karmic lens, like Little. He is as authentic as perhaps anyone I've ever met. He is dis-armingly unsophisticated and genuine to his core.

Many of these Rebuilder leaders had important inflection points on their life journeys. For Lipkis, the first was being an inspiring youth who spearheaded getting one million trees planted for the 1984 Olympics in Los Angeles. He was on Johnny Carson, made national news, and accomplished the goal of one million trees. And then he watched a great many of them die. He learned some huge lessons about stewardship and sustainability that would stick with him for the rest of his life. He went on to create an environmental nonprofit, in part based on those hard lessons learned.

Another inflection point was at the intersection of three of Los Angeles's major infrastructure agencies: Water, Sanitation, and Flood Control in the 1990s. All three were doing their jobs, taking care of the comings and goings of LA's most precious natural asset, water. Lipkis started to see something from his 24-7 Authenticity lens that none of them could quite see on their own. Eventually he got them to sit down together and realize that the amount of water one department was sending out of LA each day was about the same amount the other department was short of to meet the needs of the city.

Andy Lipkis

Lipkis shepherded an approach to using integrated watershed management to apply a forest's "natural infrastructure services" to cities. The result: a sustainable water supply, as well as flood and pollution prevention. The only way to get three conflicting parties to the table like that was to come from a place of genuine, transparent authenticity. It changes the room and creates a reliable, static-resistant channel for trust amongst all those parties.

Andy Lipkis began planting trees to rehabilitate smog- and fire-damaged areas when he was fifteen years old. He founded Tree-People, which became an international guiding light for the citizen forestry movement and sustainable urban ecosystems. You might think it all comes naturally to Lipkis. And yet, he will tell you he is constantly confronted by opportunities to *not* be authentic. He has to fight the sometimes cautious, occasionally fearful, way he processes that internal conflict to maintain his authenticity.

Whether you see karma as a real thing (like Lipkis) or metaphorically (like me), it is a powerful force that keeps him centered.

If he violated his authenticity, through lying or cutting corners, it would inevitably come back on him as negative consequences. Living with authenticity, for him, isn't a fixed equation but one that is dynamic, constantly being challenged. It needs strong feedback loops to keep in balance. Every one of these 24-7 Authenticity leaders has some sort of internal compass, in different forms, that keeps them centered.

Here is authenticity, master's level, in Lipkis's words: "The forces that keep me in check, aside from human feedback, are fully linked to my telling the truth. Thus, having the power/integrity of the universe driving the daily miracles. I don't want to lose access to that, and focusing on my authenticity is the best and only way to keep the flow going. I believe that it requires speaking fundamental truths, as those are like natural laws. I also realize that I tell and morph stories, and it's critical to keep doing truth/reality checks to keep them in integrity. The intention is always there for truth. I'm usually transparent about sharing and publicly correcting something when I find I got it wrong."

Organization-Less Leaders

With everyone in this book, I tried to make sure not only that they were a clear exemplar of a vital trait but that their stories brought forward lessons learned we could all apply. In Richard Woo's case, one vital lesson is how he maintains his sense of self across his work. For some leaders it's a simple yet powerful mental checklist; for others it's about clear core values, and for Woo, it's mindfulness. That is, paying attention to the present moment, person, or situation so as to access the "the most powerful tool available to me, myself," to be of service.

When he is working through a leadership challenge in real time, Woo consciously slows down. He tries to connect with what and who is directly in front of him, and listens first. That is how his leadership shows up. He believes the power of stillness and presence creates openings for new thinking and behavior in self and others. He is living by a personal mission statement of "building whole, affirming,

Richard Woo

and just community through deep listening, reflecting, and storytelling."

In the 1990s at Levi Strauss & Co., Woo played a lead role in the design and implementation of the company's global sourcing guidelines. These were the first-ever standards for responsible manufacturing in the apparel industry and a model for authentic corporate social responsibility (CSR) initia-

tives across private sector America. He designed and launched Project Change, a ten-year antiracism funding initiative by Levi Strauss in select communities of the American South and Southwest. He was ahead of his time more than once. He also served as the executive director of the Levi Strauss Foundation, overseeing global grantmaking in forty countries focused on economic development, HIV/AIDS, and social justice. Woo's mindfulness fit very well inside the boundaries of corporate America.

From 2000 to 2020, Woo next served as the founding CEO of the Russell Family Foundation[4] in Washington State. In leading the start-up foundation, he worked alongside the staff, family trustees, and community leaders to pioneer initiatives in Puget Sound restoration and watershed conservation, grassroots leadership, impact investing, and fossil fuel divestment/sustainable reinvestment. He left the Russell Family Foundation in January 2020, and in its 2019 awards, Inside Philanthropy named Woo the "Foundation President We'll Miss the Most" for having "been a trailblazer in such areas as equity and impact investing."

His most lasting legacy of 24-7 Authenticity may well be the Puyallup Watershed Initiative (PWI), a new model for community-centered change. They believe everyone has something to contribute to our shared home. The PWI brings together people not typically at the same table to equally address the region's persistent challenges and opportunities. So far, it's in seventeen cities, with $62 million raised and 150 nonprofit, private, and public partners. It could make you wonder why I didn't put him with cross-sector fluent Rebuilders.

One other fascinating concept Woo introduced me to is the notion of "organization-less leaders." This certainly applies to cross-sector Rebuilders who have to work across organizations, by definition. But it also broadens the idea of what leadership means. He believes we need to activate leaders at all levels of society who are not bound by traditional structures or mindsets. Much of our mental model for leadership is someone leading a particular organization as CEO or executive director or some such. That simpler, boxed-in world is less and less relevant as people like Debbie Little, Herb Virgo (in *Generosity Mindset*), and others are already demonstrating.

The scale, scope, and complexity of the megachallenges ahead will require us to reframe what a leader looks like and how they show up in the world. Richard Woo is someone leaders for the 2020s can look to for guidance.

Where Does 24-7 Authenticity Fit in Nature versus Nurture?

One of the valid questions that arises in lots of leadership books is how much can be taught and developed versus how much is largely innate, something you're just born with (or not). In general, we all agree by now that leadership can be taught; it can be learned. But within that big container of leadership, there are traits that may be more or less developable, more or less innate. Picture a continuum with a high degree of nurture on the left end and nature on the other end. 24-7 Authenticity is the trait at the midpoint—that is, the highest combination of both nature and nurture. You need lots of both.

If we apply this continuum to other vital traits, the easiest trait to develop, i.e., nurture, is Cross-Sector Fluency. Professionals can intentionally decide to take on meaningful, not cursory, roles in all three sectors, either early or over the course of their careers. Perhaps there is some inborn mindset that goes with the trait of Data Conviction, but much of it can be nurtured as well. On the other end, I think Complexity Capacity is largely something you're born with or not (see Dan Cardinali). A Generosity Mindset is primarily nature, but like 24-7 Authenticity, it typically involves some nurture as well to be fully developed.

Competitive Advantage

She was late from a call with the commissioner of the WNBA. As in all sports in the spring of 2020, she was trying to figure out how to restart a season. If I said her name was Gregg Popovich, the General Manager & Coach of the San Antonio Spurs (and you gave a darn about the NBA), you might know how whipsawed she was at the time. And of course, you'd know her if you are a WNBA fan. I'm waiting on the line, and she picks up and says, "I've been so looking forward to this, let's not rush it. I love talking about team." At this point, I'm thinking the person on the other end of the line is either laughingly disingenuous or as sincere and authentic as could be.

Alisha Valavanis is the general manager and CEO of the Seattle Storm, the local WNBA franchise. They own the distinction of being four-time WNBA world champions, most recently in the fall of 2020, in the Orlando bubble. Go Storm! Valavanis is a leadership junkie; she can't get enough. She talks to her team constantly about being authentic, how critical that trait is for high-performing teams. She thinks the "greatest competitive advantage is to be you."

Because of her workplace, Valavanis has to think about authenticity from a team standpoint from the get-go. The team is the product. In that context, she believes "authenticity is your only shot at truly leading." That's the way each teammate can stand on her own and be a leader. That's an important thread.

An even more important thread, in her mindset, is how individual authenticity leads to the optimal team capacity. Unless each person is fully authentic to who they are, you will not maximize all of the now-well-known benefits of diverse thinking and a diversity of people on a team. That goes for sports, at work, in your community.

Alisha Valavanis

The Rebuilders you're reading about live their authenticity, but Alisha thinks and strategizes on authenticity as deeply as anyone. For her, authenticity doesn't end when her players hit the floor for a game; in a very real sense, their authenticity is amplified even more when it's game time.

How does that off-the-court authenticity translate to on-the-court teamwork? A few Doug Baldwin–type notes here. When you create authenticity, everyone is more willing to trust and be vulnerable and share those feelings. That leads naturally to people more willing to share the ball. Completing the cycle, if everyone on the team is more willing to pass, they know the ball is going to come back to them, too. That may sound warm and fuzzy, but does it matter?

In the last five to ten years, basketball has seen two significant trends. First is keeping the ball moving, getting into a rhythm, which creates more spacing and better scoring opportunities. That's exactly what Valavanis's culture of authenticity optimizes. They also have the data, and conviction about it, that backs up that on-court approach. Second, there's much less rigidity in players having only one position. One player is far more likely to play multiple positions or just not have a specific, narrow role at all. You sort of have position-less teammates, which means you have leaders all over the floor, much like Richard Woo's organization-less leaders.

One last thread to Valavanis's story, similar to other Rebuilders, is how her upbringing, in part, set her on the path she's following today. She is an identical twin and one of six children. They had to work as a team; everyone's role had to be unique and valued. She's not the only person with a big family, but it just demonstrates how the journey we take in life sometimes makes more and more sense when we look back on where we came from. For Valavanis, the team started from the very beginning.

The Downside of Authenticity

Just to be sure we are speaking the same language, *downside* is defined as "an aspect or version of something that is unwanted." Every one of these five traits has a downside, a cost, an unwanted aspect that comes with the territory. In some cases, like 24-7 Authenticity, the downsides may be somewhat obvious. I think there are two main ones to consider: personal exposure and professional cost.

Personal exposure is just that, putting yourself out there for the world to see. You need to be okay with that, and it's not for everyone. I think leaders have to be at a stage and in a place in their careers in which they are okay with the risk. In Michael McAfee's case, that is pretty much who he is. For others, their authenticity might be very genuine but it comes to them over a longer time frame. In Debbie Little's story above, I don't know that she was being inauthentic, but for many years, she wasn't ready to put herself out there. If she had done so before her mind and heart were right, it would have crashed for her.

Richard Woo is in tune with a different personal cost: being vulnerable. He is a guy who can't hide his feelings; he has spent his whole life being deeply present and mindful. When he does bring his authentic self, he can pay a personal cost, the cost of being a deeply vulnerable leader.

The potential professional cost is much like McAfee's career getting detoured when he spoke the truth or Trish Millines having to jump off a career track to pursue the work that needed to be done. Not everyone, everywhere values authenticity, genuine authenticity. You will sometimes have a choice to "give in" to that less than authentic part of the culture of your company, your organization, your neighborhood.

We all make personal and professional choices every day. Our depth and degree of authenticity is a summation of all those individual decisions and choices. You are constantly building up your account balance of authenticity or making withdrawals (or going bankrupt). While it's fairly easy to go bankrupt, it's very hard to have a full account, and even harder to keep the balance full.

Not the Guy Who Rides Bikes

This isn't about the famous guy in this picture. Doug Ulman was the CEO of Livestrong at the time Lance Armstrong was making his comeback. On October 2, 1996, at age twenty-five, Armstrong was diagnosed with advanced testicular cancer. It had spread to his lymph nodes, lungs, brain, and abdomen. The prognosis was not good, but he made an incredible recovery. Armstrong's comeback and seven Tour de France wins were amazing and inspiring for millions. It led to the creation of Livestrong and made the yellow wrist band ubiquitous for many years. After a few false starts, the first outside CEO Armstrong hired to lead Livestrong was Ulman, himself a three-time cancer survivor.

Other than "just" founding a 501(c)(3) nonprofit, while in college, to provide support to young adults who are affected by cancer, Ulman had no previous organizational leadership experience. Five years out of college, in 2004, he found himself the president of the Livestrong Foundation, a global, eight-figure budget enterprise. It was quite a ride with incredible growth and the building of a global movement.

Fast-forward nine years to the moment everything changed. In an interview with Oprah on January 17, 2013, Armstrong confessed that he had used banned performance-enhancing drugs throughout  much of his cycling career. That doping helped him to each of his seven wins. We know what publicly played out with Armstrong in the subsequent months. He was vilified. What about the president of the organization that millions of people poured their hopes and fears (and resources) into and that now, for some, was a secondhand symbol of Armstrong's betrayal?

Doug Ulman

Ulman was faced with one of the most extreme, visible leadership challenges any leader, from any sector, would ever want to face. The details and outcomes about Lance Armstrong are fairly well known. Far less known is the incredible leadership Ulman exhibited. He had to bring a wide range of leadership traits to bear, with not much experience to lean on. The paramount attribute that defined him was 24-7 Authenticity.

He was open, honest, and transparent at every turn, unlike Armstrong had been for years. Authenticity that largely maintained the faith in and brand of Livestrong, and kept the organization strong throughout. It was an amazing accomplishment under the circumstances.

"In a crisis, you are working with very imperfect information," Ulman told me, "and for a while everything is negative." So how do you get from negativity to realism to inspiration? Ulman not only had millions of Livestrong believers outside the company who were confused at best, but he also had about a hundred staff internally who were reeling.

The primary capital a leader has at that moment is trust. That trust is built, first and foremost, through the authenticity of the leader. In moments of crisis, leaders effectively have to spend that capital. If they haven't built up enough capital at that moment, the organization and the cause can go bankrupt, morally as well as financially.

Ulman not only had built enough capital to "spend down"; he also increased his trust capital by how he showed up over and over. The value of his authenticity grew even greater during that crisis. I almost ended up taking Ulman's place when he left, after he guided the organization through all of the storms, so I've gotten to know him a bit. With many of these 24-7 leaders, their authenticity shows up about ten seconds into your first conversation with them. Ulman is no exception.

Ten Things We Know about 24-7 Authenticity Leaders for the Future

1. Many of them found, organically or intentionally, a handful of mentors along their journeys. Very specifically, not pat-you-on-the-back or technical-skill-developing or have-a-beer mentors, but truth-telling, accountability-creating mentors who were themselves emblematic of authenticity.
2. There is absolutely a cost to 24-7 Authenticity. It is not free. You will not go through your career without paying that real cost more than once (or, if you don't, you probably haven't held up to your standards).
3. Look for the data, or people with Data Conviction, to come alongside your 24-7 Authenticity. They are very mutually reinforcing and make the combination greater than 1+1=2.

4. These Rebuilders have some sort of tangible, simple powerful values list or North Star that keeps them grounded and that they return to frequently, especially when times get tough.

5. Some, not all, of these leaders are centered in some form of faith or spirituality. This exists right alongside the previous point about values and a North Star. It just takes different forms for different people.

6. They all have a strong sense of self. That doesn't mean arrogance or self-satisfaction; quite the opposite. It does mean there is a genuine internal, constant search for a truer self. You will miss the mark sometimes, and when you do, your honesty and authenticity with yourself is not optional.

7. Organizational titles, boundaries, and domains of this kind of leadership are often irrelevant or blurry. Some are organizational-less.

8. Their number-one asset is trust, and without that trust capital in a crisis, leadership can go bankrupt. Be mindful when spending down your capital, as in a crisis, that it is not an endless supply.

9. Most of those leaders are not uncaring, but their need for being liked is low. Their primacy on being understood for who they truly are is exceptionally high. If they have the latter, the former is of relatively lower consequence.

10. "What you see is what you get" can be said about every one of them.

I try to make music with emotion and integrity. And authenticity. You can feel when something's authentic, and you can feel when it's not: you know when someone's trying to make the club record, or trying to make the girl record, or trying to make the thug record. It's none of that. It's just my emotions.   —JAY-Z

CHAPTER SIX

Complexity Capacity

G iven that the total breadth and depth of challenges future leaders need to grapple with in the decade ahead are greater than we've faced, at least in the past seventy-five years (megachallenge #2), a capacity for complexity is an absolute need in any serious organization. Especially in a post-COVID world.

The capacity means you not only have to be able to take in the many variables at play, but interpret, process, and make sense of them, and ultimately communicate effectively. This trait is very much about using both sides of your brain.

Complexity can scare many people away. I think this is the most innate of the five vital traits. I would say you can increase someone's capacity in degrees through specific professional development. Some will grow their capacity incrementally through experience (that fits me). But I don't think you can take anyone from amateur to expert, and you certainly can't take anyone from no capacity to high capacity. It just rarely works that way. There almost always has to be some innate capacity.

Complexity Capacity benefits from an open heart and strategic mind, aka a Generosity Mindset, to put that intricate understanding to work. You will see that duality at play many times in the next two chapters and dozen or so leaders.

 THE MOST COMPLEX type of bridge, in general, is a truss bridge, one whose load-bearing structure is a series of connected elements usually forming triangular units. A truss bridge can handle the biggest loads and has the greatest capacity in bridge designs. Some Rebuilders are uniquely suited to have this innate capacity to understand and interpret the complexity around them and take on the biggest loads.

Any darn fool can make something complex; it takes a genius to make something simple.   —PETE SEEGER

What Could Be More Complex Than Leading a Tech Start-Up Back in the 1980s?

When she was the first chief communications officer at AOL, working alongside founder Steve Case, Kathy Calvin "only had one primary shareholder." Investors in a private sector start-up are not exactly cupcakes or easy sells, but they are pretty straightforward. It's show-me-the-money, and the more of it the better.

After a long and, by any measure, effective career at AOL, Calvin moved on to a workplace with a few more "shareholders," the United

Nations Foundation (UNF). A lot of what she learned at AOL applied at UNF. One thing she couldn't fully prepare for was the range and degree of the complexity of a role like the CEO of UNF, where she served for ten years. She is the first one to admit that the govern-

Kathy Calvin

ment probably moves the slowest of the sectors; that's kind of the way it was designed. It's also where some of the biggest change happens.

Over her tenure, Calvin oversaw the transition from the first Millennium Development Goals, focused on ending poverty, to the broader Sustainable Development Goals, aimed at building prosperity and op-

portunity. Not only did this make the goals more actionable and measurable, but even more importantly, it made them usable by the private and nonprofit sectors, not just governments.

That's a huge shift that reflects her private sector background, and the shift made cross-sector partnerships much more possible and her Cross-Sector Fluency so much more valuable. Calvin reflected on the value of different forms of capital in this work. The scarcity of capital was human, not financial, in her work at UNF, not something you would expect a nonprofit leader to say. Calvin is also not your typical nonprofit leader.

Her career spanned work in the public, private, and nonprofit sectors, and she is a passionate advocate for multisector problem solving. Like more than one Rebuilder, she could have been connected to another trait, Cross-Sector Fluency, just as easily. When I ran a draft of this by her, she had an interesting reflection: "AOL always had a measure of social impact as well—governments, consumers, and those whose lives we improved through connectivity. That movement has only grown, since AOL was an early champion of a company with purpose." Sounds like the kind of person that would be a leader for social change no matter where she is.

A Definition of Capacity for Complexity

We've already talked about a number of factors making our world more complex:

- ▶ the blurring of the private, public, and nonprofit sectors
- ▶ the increasing inequity of and silos between our citizens
- ▶ the sheer breadth and depth of the challenges we are facing

This trait is about the ability to process all of those variables and more. Can you not only see, take in, and process them, but can you also interpret them and make progress, like every one of the Rebuilders you will read about in this section?

Complexity Capacity is about being and thinking in a nonlinear, less sequential way. It's about knowing that past solutions may be decreasingly useful for informing future solutions, hence the need to rethink and rebuild. It's about adaptability and being able to take in new information constantly. Complexity Capacity means, metaphorically, that you are better at open-ended essay questions on the "test" than multiple choice or true-false.

Last but not least, listening as a core asset and attribute of leadership has always been a "special sauce" in my recipe for leadership. That skill, active listening, as Mike Myatt of N2 Growth[1] defines it, is the act of genuinely listening, not just to hear or to be ready to respond, but wholly leaning in and fully understanding what others are saying. It's not hard to understand how vital active listening is as a characteristic of leaders with a high Complexity Capacity.

Complexity . . . True Complexity

Complexity is running the UN Foundation? Yes. Complexity is navigating the $2 trillion CARES Act on behalf of the nonprofit sector?

Certainly. But complexity, true complexity . . . is being homeless with three young sons. And navigating your way back, all the way back to where you are "committed to making sure other parents see and exercise their power from their position and place." That is Erica Valliant's definition and life experience of complexity. It is part of her story that makes her a real leader today and for the future.

Erica Valliant

That wasn't the only time she navigated complexity. Without a bachelor's degree, she educated herself to have the expertise and certification to trade stocks, bonds, and securities. Then she got laid off. She navigated her way through being temporarily homeless and got her family firmly back on solid ground. When you read her career progression from there, it spans policy advocate to community engagement leader to whole family systems manager to organizer, activist, and mother.

Since she doesn't have a title like CEO or executive director or mayor (yet), she won't usually find her way into books on leadership. And yet she is exactly the kind of future leader that has the Complexity Capacity we are going to need badly. Go back to our definition—the ability to take in, process, and interpret variables and make progress; being and thinking in a nonlinear, less sequential way; being able to adapt and take in new information constantly. Valliant checks all of those criteria in a substantive way.

I can't stress enough that the challenges we face in the decade ahead are going to take leaders in untraditional places, at all levels of communities and companies, and with a wide variety of experiences and skill sets. Valliant's LinkedIn profile doesn't even list half of the roles and job titles she's held over the last twenty-plus years.

How does that breadth and depth of experiences affect one's perspective on community change? Valliant said it has made her more patient with people and able to hear and see multiple perspectives on all sides of an issue. In addition to her own lived experiences, she said she's always been fascinated by human psychology. She likes looking at things through a human-centered lens, always making sure to step back and see the whole picture, and making sure the right conversations happen. She also credits her uncle, as she was growing up, who had a master's in math and would talk often and long with her about topics from physics to family.

Here's maybe the most important value of a leader like Valliant—often, she is the one in the room with the broadest range of life experiences, quite often not easy ones and often outside the norm. When she thinks about how real change happens, she thinks we need more people outside the norm at the table. She asked me, eloquently, "How can we infiltrate the places where change needs to happen if the people at the table don't have those experiences?" She finds herself often in the role of interpreter, of being a Sherpa. That's what leaders with a capacity for complexity can do.

Complexity? Being homeless with three little boys is a complexity most of us have never had to conceive of navigating, much less surviving and then thriving. Erica also grew up in a house with no windows, just boards; her mother was diagnosed with HIV when Erica was fourteen and she watched her die the next year, when her mom was thirty-three; her little brother died when she was seven and he was five months old; and Erica's dad died when she was nineteen, from heart failure, when he was forty years old. Just surviving is more than a lot of people could have mustered. Becoming a community leader after all of that—hard to fathom.

You need to make real progress on homelessness? Leaders like Valliant must be at that table. You need someone who can interface between the community and policy makers? Valliant is a first-rate candidate. You need someone who understands the corporate world and the street? Erica Valliant does. She is a unique Rebuilder. The amount of experiences and challenges and knowledge she has now accumulated in her life and career are a powerful asset. We need to find more Rebuilders like Valliant and more ways for them to lead.

You Better Have Women in the Room

The specific places and people don't matter, but I can just tell you I lived a lesson too many times. Something has become increasingly clear to me, especially the last five years as an independent consultant. It's very clear to me, empirically. It's a fact.

If you have a complex, multivariate, hard-to-define, multistakeholder, big, gnarly problem to solve, you better have enough women in the room. That's not a universal statement about all women and all men, but on the whole, it's true. I'll acknowledge right up front that this is a male perspective on women, so I hope you'll accept my intent as authentic, if not perfect.

I've been in too many meetings and projects in which the women were better at thinking through all the variables, processing the issues, and making them make some sense. Frankly, they are also way better at getting their egos out of the way and keeping focused on the ultimate, best possible solution to the problem at hand. And the more complex the problem, the more egos can get in the way.

This could have been a whole chapter unto itself. When I ran early drafts of this point of view by some good friends, I got responses (from both genders) all over the gamut from "I love that you are talking about this," to "Why make it about women specifically; isn't that some stereotype?" to "You're just trying to be politically correct." So I'll just let the chips fall where they may.

To be explicit, I've been in many situations in which because certain men were in the room, or only men or mostly men, failure was created when there could have been success. There is never a one-size-fits-all statement, but it's played out this way too many times, sometimes very frustratingly so. To my fellow guys I'd say, it's time to completely get rid of the relic of the boys' club; it just doesn't work as well anymore—and probably never did.

More than one headline in the spring of 2020 basically said that countries led by women have fared better against coronavirus.[2] Why? The consensus is that women leaders are better able to demonstrate a balance of strength and compassion, which due to societal expectations placed on both genders is easier said than done.

Kathleen Gersen, a professor of sociology at New York University, suggests that a fully developed leader should be both strong and capable of feeling. She says, "If women can lead the way in showing that these are not competing and conflicting attributes, but are in fact complementary and necessary for good leadership, I think not only will society benefit, but so will men. Maybe then we can begin to open up the scripts for roles that leaders play, regardless of whether it's a woman or a man or anything else."[3]

This line of thinking has made me try to figure out if there is some science-based reason why this dynamic—women having a greater capacity for complexity—could be true. Especially over the last twenty years, there has been more and more research done on this question. Specifically, on how male and female brains differ.

In the '90s, two of the first researchers to venture into this space were Diane Halpern, PhD, past president of the American Psychological Association, and Nirao Shah, now a Stanford professor of psychiatry and behavioral sciences and neurobiology. Lots of other research followed from other good sources. There is still debate, but in a meta-analysis done by Stanford Medicine a few years ago,[4] here are a few findings that seem to be widely held and relevant for us:

▶ Maybe most fundamentally, the two hemispheres of a
   woman's brain talk to each other more than a man's do. In
   a 2014 study, University of Pennsylvania researchers
   imaged the brains of 428 male and 521 female youths, an

uncharacteristically huge sample. They found that females' brains consistently showed more strongly coordinated activity between hemispheres. The males' brain activity was more tightly coordinated within local brain regions.

▶ A woman's hippocampus, critical to learning and memorization, is larger than a man's and works differently. A man's amygdala, associated with the experiencing of emotions and the recollection of such experiences, is bigger than a woman's.

▶ Women excel in several measures of verbal ability, pretty much all of them, except for verbal analogies. Women's reading comprehension and writing ability consistently exceed that of men, on average. They're more adept at retrieving information from long-term memory.

▶ In adulthood, women remain more oriented to faces, men to things.

Every one of those findings, subtly or overtly, speak to a great Complexity Capacity. One of the summative comments in the meta-analysis was that "all the measured differences are averages derived from pooling widely varying individual results. While *statistically significant*, the differences tend not to be *gigantic*." That sounds about right. Men have plenty of positive attributes, but a capacity for complexity is not at the top of the list.

I was on an excellent webinar in April 2020, looking at scenario planning and how businesses should rethink the future due to COVID. The speaker was Mark Johnson,[5] cofounder, with Clayton Christenson, of the consulting firm Innosight. One of the topics, understandably, was about complexity and how to deal with it. I sent a comment on the chat and talked with him a few weeks later. I suggested the premise of this section and asked what his perspective was. He was clear that his opinion was based on experiences and anecdotes, not a formal analysis of any kind.

To the question of women being better at and having a greater capacity for complexity, he said simply, "Yes, that's been my anecdotal experience on the whole. They tend to be more right-brained, creative, imaginative, and able to think at higher levels of abstraction."

At the end of the day, this can be accurately conjoined with the overall issue of diversity in work teams, community groups, executive-level leadership, and so on. The research on that broader idea is a little more conclusive these days. In a 2015 analysis,[6] McKinsey & Company's summation was "companies in the top quartile for gender or racial and ethnic diversity are more likely to have financial returns above their national industry medians. Diversity is probably a competitive differentiator that shifts market share toward more diverse companies over time."

Why would that be the case? Because "more diverse companies are better able to win top talent and improve their customer orientation, employee satisfaction, and decision-making, and all that leads to a virtuous cycle of increasing returns." Is that enough yet?

As we said earlier, diversity aimed at a shared purpose, not merely diversity for diversity's sake. Diversity already is. It exists. It's the reality of America. For it to be optimized, diversity needs to be empowered with a common goal or interest. In terms of problem-solving, without a sense of shared purpose, a diverse team can fail to deliver progress, just like any other ill-conceived team. The diversity I'm focused on here is women in the room. Of course, it applies to people of color and other categories, too. Diversity like the thirty-eight Rebuilders you are reading about.

I need to briefly touch on one more question: Why aren't women just naturally "in the room" more often to bring that greater capacity for complexity to the table of problem-solving? In groundbreaking and very current research[7] at BYU, Brittany Karford Rogers reports that "for women, having a seat at the table does not always mean having a voice. Women are systematically seen as less authoritative, and their influence is systematically lower. . . . They're speaking less. And when they're speaking up, they're not being listened to as much, and they are being interrupted more." Not to mention the all-too-frequent dynamics of man-splaining and he-peating.

However inadvertent, the gender dynamics shutting women down are real, says Jennifer Preece, BYU associate professor of political science.[8] The environment, she emphasizes, doesn't have to be hostile. Rather than outright misogyny, she says it's usually cultural norms and gendered messages that subtly, and profoundly, shape the rules of engagement. Individuals who suppress female speech may do so unwittingly. We have lots of learning and unlearning to do.

Let's leave it at this. The next time you are part of a meeting or a team trying to solve a complex problem, putting together a group to take on a significant challenge, or in a situation where you know the problem to be solved is not obvious or simple, look around the room. Are there enough women in the room? I didn't say only women (100 percent of either gender is likely suboptimal). If you have only men in the room, I hope your problem or challenge is simple or insignificant. And, after all, are there really many simple, insignificant problems left for the 2020s? Not many.

> I am not gonna have any more meetings that aren't at least a third women. —MARC BENIOFF, founder and CEO, Salesforce.com

Flag Waver and Bridge Builder

I'm not unbiased when it comes to Sudha Nandagopal, the CEO of Social Venture Partners International,[9] the global network of thousands of civic and philanthropic leaders in forty-plus cities in eight countries. She is also one of those leaders who could have fit in multiple places in this story. To start with, she has a pretty sophisticated lens on complexity. She is one of a small number of leaders I know that can wave a flag (i.e., take a strong hard position) and build a bridge (be the person who can bring the flag wavers to the table together). What you soon learn is she is playing the connector, convener role, but not from any passive point of view. She plays the long game.

Her capacity comes from, in part, working with all three sectors: public (City of Seattle Equity and Environment Initiative cofounder),

Sudha Nandagopal

private (Corporate Accountability International, which activates people to challenge and change corporations), and nonprofit (Washington Conservation Voters communications manager, board member at One America, and Social Ventures Partners International CEO).

One of the powerful things Nandagopal conveyed to me was that she has to work with a lot of people who have a lot of depth in one area, but "issues and solutions are not in silos." That sticks with me. Issues and challenges in the twentieth century sometimes fit in silos, but very few of them will in the decade ahead.

She also has a master's-level view on how the private sector needs to think about how they can play a more community-based, stakeholder-driven role. Two quick examples. Amazon contributing to a charitable fund? Important, but not that big of a deal for systemic change. How they treat their workers and the precedent it sets? That matters big-time. And the private sector making sure community organizations have a seat at the tables of power they routinely sit at? Good. Corporations understanding where they are situated in a community and how they are accountable and responsible to that community? That matters.

She brings an intellectually rigorous mindset to the work she does. She is always scoping and surveying. She looks for common ground while not asking anyone to give up their ground carelessly, which leads to more sustainable solutions. She is willing to risk her professional capital, when the right opportunity presents, for the larger good. Don't expect Nandagopal to follow the crowd, but do expect her to lead by bringing the crowd together.

I Love an "Emergency"

Rahm Emanuel's rather famous quote is "never let a crisis go to waste." Aaron Hurst takes that one step further: he "loves" an emergency, a crisis. How could that be? If you knew him, you'd

have a good inkling why. He is a creative, out-of-the-box thinker, the kind of leader you absolutely need involved in complex situations . . . but not the only kind you need.

You may know Hurst's name from his book *The Purpose Economy*. He is one of the true thought leaders in the evolution of purpose in corporate America, which we'll

Aaron Hurst

talk about later in Cross-Sector Fluency. He is an entrepreneur at heart and soul. Today he is the CEO of Imperative, a peer-coaching platform for leaders, of course.

He loves emergencies because they are an opportunity for a leader to create new signals and a new path forward. It's easy to be a good leader 90 percent of the time, by his way of thinking, but the great ones figure out the complexity and adjust to it quickly and keep adjusting and readjusting in that other 10 percent.

Hurst is the kind of person who will tell you he is comfortable with ambiguity and with being wrong. And he believes the kind of leaders we need right now are the ones with the greatest combination of agility and humanity. That distills down to a useful checklist when thinking about how to develop yourself or assess your abilities:

- ▶ Be comfortable with ambiguity and with being wrong.
- ▶ Learn to like change and always be curious.
- ▶ Have a combination of agility and humanity.

I'll take it another step. Hurst is a guy I like a lot, but you don't want too many Hursts in the room either. Tolerance for ambiguity or affinity for change like his, *in excess,* on your team(s) doesn't grow your capacity for complexity; it can diffuse it. All five of these vital traits have their own idiosyncrasies. Perhaps not surprisingly, Complexity Capacity may be the most difficult trait to find and deploy of any of the five.

The Downside of Capacity for Complexity

I'll say I sometimes suffer from the downside of complexity, the inability to simplify the understanding and processing of complex problems. That doesn't mean oversimplification or dumbing it down. One of the challenges with a vital trait like this is that it's equally about processing the inputs and producing the outputs. That's why this one stands out as likely the one that is most inherent, part of someone's DNA, more nature than nurture. This takes some unique brain capacity.

There are fewer downsides, per se, to this trait, but it is probably the most unique one and the hardest to transfer. If you can find these leaders with a high capacity for complexity, keep 'em. You need to make sure you have enough team members with this trait, and the more complex the problem, the higher capacity you need.

Don't Hit Send

There is an opportunity gap in education in America, and making progress to close this gap has been difficult and often erratic. What we are now starting to grasp, urgently and clearly, is that the opportunity gap is growing with every passing day, week, and month that children are not in school due to COVID. The acceleration of an increasingly unequal America over the last twenty years, as we discussed back in chapter 2, is being amplified by COVID in perhaps no greater place than public education.

One of the few entities that has made tangible progress to close the education achievement gap, at a measurable level and in a sustained way, is StriveTogether.[10] Working to achieve racial and ethnic equity, StriveTogether knows that when a community prioritizes helping every child succeed, it brings us all one step closer to an equitable world. Across their national network, local partnerships are improving outcomes at major milestones: thirty-one of their communities in kindergarten readiness, forty-three in middle-grade math, and fifteen in employment readiness.

The complexity of the education system comes up many times in this book. The key lesson from someone like Jennifer Blatz, president and CEO of StriveTogether, is how she effectively manages and copes with complexity. As a leader, she must be clear about the intended results while navigating complexity.

Jennifer Blatz

Simple enough, right? Well, what's actually simpler is having the private sector North Star of net profit. In today's world, either by intention or by necessity, looking at one, single bottom line isn't going to cut it anymore. Leaders like Blatz have already dealt with the complexity of more than one bottom line and more than one result. That dilemma, that complexity, is native to leaders like her; and more future leaders will need this quality.

Here's an interesting and simple tool she uses to manage, digest, and ultimately translate complexity. She writes emails that she doesn't send. Let's explain. Achieving outcomes in education ultimately relies on outcomes from other sectors, such as housing, food security, or transportation. This means sifting through volumes of information to reveal the root cause of an issue, then pulling the levers that can change the outcomes. To do this requires a number of tools and approaches including cross-sector collaboration, root-cause analysis, and risk management, among others.

As such, the simple act of organizing her ideas and thoughts on "paper" (email-to-be-sent) helps Blatz sharpen her thinking and make sense of the complexity. It also helps her to plan out the optimum next steps, whether finding the best way to direct her team, deciding when to push more aggressively toward a goal or to back off for the time being, or when to draw on knowledge experts who can provide new insights. Drafting it as an email-to-be-sent makes it more real, more personal. It's one simple, but powerful tool for distilling and processing complexity.

I love this story because Blatz has a big brain; she has to deal with the whole education system. But she has a simple way to help her distill and organize at least some of complexity she deals with. It's a cool example of how a leader simplifies complexity, not just for herself, but everyone around her.

Eight Things We Know about Capacity for Complexity Leaders for the Future

1. People best at complexity also tend to have meaningful cross-sector experience. It helps all of the complexity

make more sense and makes it a little easier to bring it all together.

2. Make sure you look at the balance in the makeup on your team. You certainly don't want to have a lack of complexity teammates, but you also don't want to have too many.

3. There are traits to look for that reflect higher complexity capacity, like comfort with ambiguity and change while having no less humanity.

4. To create clarity and centeredness in the complexity, it's vital that a leader have a set of strong clear values that are persistently, not intermittently, applied.

5. Be cautious about assuming you can transfer or teach this capacity for complexity. It's hard to do.

6. Wherever you lie on this complexity continuum, find ways to get outside your comfort zone and normal domains to expand your own capacity.

7. Don't tackle a complex problem without enough women in the room.

8. And remember, Complexity Capacity needs a Generosity Mindset alongside it in order to put that intricate understanding to work with and for real people.

We don't have a public that really understands the world anymore, and in an age of complexity, that problem becomes more difficult.

—ZBIGNIEW BRZEZINSKI

CHAPTER SEVEN

Generosity Mindset

When we are less connected and more siloed and isolated, and our ability to come together is harder today than it perhaps ever has been (megachallenge #3), the openness and expansiveness of a Generosity Mindset becomes vital. This might be the hardest trait to put into practice persistently and with fidelity.

Whatever the social or economic or health disparities at hand, it is going to require a range of people and perspectives and philosophies. The ability to be the leader that, as Rosanne Haggerty said, creates a commitment to unity and looks for what you can commonly share while respecting each other's differences is pivotal. The mindset to leave room for multiple identities at just about all costs is paramount.

And remember that a Generosity Mindset needs to be able to process complexity in order to know where and how opportunities arise that can be leveraged and sustained.

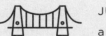 JUST LIKE THE superstructure on a bridge, a Generosity Mindset might appear to be the least structurally important. But like a cantilever bridge, it is fundamental to the whole structure and strength of the bridge being rebuilt. It might seem to be just a more visually appealing element, but it's far more than that. Those leaders with a Generosity Mindset might not be as obviously structural and strategic to the ultimate solution, but they are sometimes the piece that makes all the parts come together.

This is the fight that we wage. Against ourselves and each other. Because America is not natural. Natural is tribal. We're fighting against thousands of years of human behavior. To create something that no one's ever done. So that's what's exceptional about America. Like this ain't easy. —JON STEWART

Generosity as Strategy

Every once in a while, you talk to one of these leaders and you're a little mesmerized by their words. There isn't a whole lot of editing or added storytelling needed. The leader's words say all that's

Cecilia Gutierrez

needed to say. Cecilia Gutierrez is one of those leaders. A little like Michael Smith, she embodies and lives with a spirit and mindset of generosity.

Gutierrez "tilts the room." That phrase refers to those who just change things by their presence. It's more commonly used to describe someone with charisma or power or who just commands the room (usually, not always, in good ways). Cecilia Gutierrez tilts the room because, in her words, she uses a "Generosity Mindset as strategy." When I asked her how she thinks about her role in a meeting, a group, a team, she gave a crystal clear, nonhesitant answer. She said her mindset is about three core beliefs:

She only does work where she has a deep belief in the "power and promise of the work." As she was saying that, an interesting notion came to mind. Showing up as often as she has over the years, she doesn't have to go searching for work that has real purpose and meaning anymore. It finds her.

Gutierrez believes that every single person in the room has something to contribute. She finds the space for each person's contribution to show up. Stop and truly think about those two sentences for a minute. When is the last time you were in an organizational meeting when at least one person had that amount of true, authentic generosity in her or his approach to the work at hand? It's not very often. The effect of that deep belief is often like a hidden hand guiding the work. You might not ever notice it explicitly, but it's there and the power it has is profound and lasting.

Last but not least, Gutierrez has a core value that if we truly want to get the best out of one another, we have to be willing to openly share and be fully transparent, no matter what. That may sound sort of self-evident, but the point is that Gutierrez is thinking that way 24-7. Her way of being, her Generosity Mindset, is powerful. She is constantly scanning each person, believing it's her "job" to get the best out of everyone.

It leaves a person to wonder—how does someone like her deal with zero-sum, play-only-for-themselves people? She approaches every situation with "overwhelming optimism." She is constantly trying to make as many people as possible successful. She told me she is always trying to think about how she can communicate in a way that every person can hear it. In short, her Generosity Mindset is relentless. Over time, it crowds out the zero-sum players.

When I talk to most of these Rebuilders, there are a few common dimensions we can use to understand each of them. One of those is the degree to which their trait was nature versus nurture (we touched on it back in chapter 5), born-with-it versus learned-it-through-experience. For masters of a trait like Gutierrez, the answer is usually both. Just like Darell Hammond, who you'll read about in a moment, she didn't start out with a whole lot early in life; in fact, not much, other than the love of her mom.

Having to grow up in and eventually out of a life of poverty assuredly gave her the ingrained approach to getting the most out of others, because she didn't have as much herself. It also, earlier in her career, sometimes held her back from fully believing in her own ability to lead and from leaning into her own power. I've been in many meetings with Gutierrez, and she has clearly left those internal doubts behind (or so it appears to me).

When she is in the room, there is a better pace; when she is not, things move more circuitously. When she is in the room, there is a stronger determination and spirit; when she is not, there are more diversions and sidetracks. When she is in the room, things get done and more progress happens; when she is not, the ultimate goal seems further away.

Whether it's in your neighborhood or corporation or government, and you think about solving the scale and complexity of problems we face in the 2020s, take a look at that previous paragraph. Ask yourself, do we have our Cecilia? And if not, where can we find her/him?

A Definition of *Generosity Mindset*

Just to reemphasize, the point isn't about being nicey-nice or polite. It's a strategic mindset. It's a way of working and doing business, all the time. When you come to any setting, you are looking to see who's missing from the table and who needs to be connected. You are able to keep your eyes on the ultimate prize and get past disagreements, detours, and diversions.

Some of the best research on generosity, as a science, is done by the Templeton Foundation.[1] Its definition of generosity is more in a community or philanthropic context, but there are a handful of specific, relevant findings that give this mindset some strong underpinnings. They looked at more than 350 studies and metastudies published between 1971 and 2017, and offered this summary:

> After decades of research that assumed human nature to be intrinsically selfish and aggressive, recent years have seen the emergence of a more complex and nuanced understanding. While studies suggest that humans have a propensity for self-interest, research has also revealed that currents of generosity run deep within us.

Generosity appears to have especially strong associations with psychological health and well-being. Generosity toward others has been shown to help smooth over "relational noise"—perceived unfairness that can arise from everyday misunderstandings—making it a critical ingredient for increasing relational trust.[2]

One study found that generosity creates self-other overlap, a sense of "oneness" with others, and reasoned that, when we help others under this state of oneness, we feel as if we are also helping ourselves.

What that meta-research affirms is the need to keep a constantly open mind. Fewer and fewer people can do this today, so its unique value constantly increases. In a sense, a Generosity Mindset also requires you to have a sort of relentless authenticity.

Paying Back the Generosity You Received

How do you go through life with a hugely and openly Generous Mindset when, at least in one respect, you started out life in a far-less-than-generous set of circumstances? Darell Hammond was born to a nursing-home worker and a truck driver. Two years later,

Darell Hammond

Darell's father abandoned the family. His mother had a breakdown and found herself unable to take care of the children. He was sent to a boys' home in Illinois.

All these years later, he characterizes that fourteen-year experience two thousand miles away from his birthplace as being the "benefactor of generosity." He remembers times when there was not always enough food at the table, quite literally, to go around. When that happened, the generosity of the whole community came shining through, something not lost on Hammond for the rest of his life. There was no "tragedy of the commons" at their dinner table. He had hundreds of small inflection points in his life that shaped who he is.

Mooseheart Child City & School is a residential childcare facility, located on a thousand-acre campus thirty-eight miles west of Chicago. Dedicated more than a hundred years ago by the Loyal Order of Moose fraternal organization, Mooseheart cares for youth whose families are unable, for a wide variety of reasons, to care for them. For most of us, that is an upbringing that's hard to even relate to.

For some of Hammond's young peers, it was no doubt a hard upbringing that broke some of their spirits along the way. For Hammond, it was a place and experience that nurtured and amplified something that must have already been within him the day he was born: a Generosity Mindset.

A heartwarming story for sure, but what's the relevance to leadership in the 2020s? In an increasingly unequal and siloed world, authentic generosity is an increasingly rare and highly strategic trait in a leader. As Hammond sees it, you cannot play a zero-sum game, period. Not because doing so is the "nicer" way to be, but because playing a zero-sum game flat out loses. How would Hammond know if his no-zero-sum-game strategy works? Well, start by building a $33 million organization (nonprofit) from scratch in dozens of US cities. That's what Hammond accomplished with Kaboom.

The next question that comes out of his story is what does building a national nonprofit that advocates for the building of playgrounds and healthy play have to do with leadership for the future? If it wasn't clear before 2020, it is now. We have to have leaders that can cut across a wide range of people and places and do so in a way in which a majority of people can connect with one another.

Hammond needed all the Generosity Mindset he could muster when he dealt with private sector leaders, school principals and superintendents, and *especially* parents. The challenges included turf issues with local nonprofits already in existence, safety issues with the public sector, and the list goes on. The range of stakeholders that leaders are going to have to deal with is only getting larger as are the number of variables at play as the five megachallenges also increase. Rebuilders like Hammond have already walked that gauntlet. He knows what it takes.

Just as Michael McAfee's 24-7 Authenticity and Sondra Samuels's Data Conviction are self-evident within about ten seconds of meeting them, the same is true of Hammond's Generosity Mindset and spirit. Again, what you see with Rebuilders is oftentimes what you truly get.

The Playground in Purple Pants

The purple pants don't really have all that much to do with Maya Enista Smith's Generosity Mindset, but they do explain how her family got to the United States. The juxtaposition with Darell Hammond's story is not random.

When Smith's parents were growing up in Romania, one night her mom had a dream about playing on a "playground in purple pants." Her mom woke up and said the family had to move to the

United States, which they eventually did. Smith's family's journey and new homes around the globe are relevant to her Generosity Mindset today, even if the through line isn't 100 percent clear.

Maya Enista Smith

Smith's parents immigrated six years before she was born in New York City. Her family left Romania and came to the United States with basically nothing. They were first-generation immigrants, alone in a new country, so they had to rely on the generosity of others time and again. The point here isn't that this is a heartwarming story, which it is, but how it later shaped Smith's worldview and helped her become a truly effective leader. But it took a while.

Growing up, Smith wasn't yet someone you'd say had a Generosity Mindset. She wasn't always so friendly, probably a coping mechanism, but three events in the years after she graduated high school changed her whole mindset about the world around her.

The first was 9-11, which was also the first day of her freshman year of college. We all know where we were when we first heard about it, and it affected everyone. Maya Enista Smith decided that day that she needed to show up in the world differently. Maybe the inhumane cruelty of what she witnessed began to break through the not-so-generous girl that just graduated high school.

Next was meeting a guy who was religious, a guy she went on to marry. He had a decidedly faith-driven view of the world. That spirit sometimes carries over to your spouse. As with many Rebuilders, there are threads of spirituality and faith in Smith's story.

The third moment was at a conference listening to the keynote speaker talk about the value and importance of mentoring. She took him at his word and passed him a handwritten note (back when people did that) about being a mentor for her. The speaker, Darell Hammond, replied and said he'd be glad to.

Today, Smith says generosity is her "most core mindset about the world."

In real terms, the nonprofit sector has scarcer resources than the private or public sector. That leads many in the social sector to have a scarcity, zero-sum mindset; and over the long term, those leaders lose. She and Hammond clearly have a few common threads. More fundamentally, just like Haggerty, Hammond, Michael Smith, and Guiterrez, Maya Smith wins with a Generosity Mindset, in her case because of three factors:

1. It cuts through the unequal, siloed noise and dissonance. Her unique value proposition as a leader is greater and increasing.
2. It attracts great people to your team, great investors, and high-value networks and relationships that you can leverage forever, as long as there is generous reciprocity.
3. It sells, whether the customer is "buying" from a nonprofit with a donation or a consumer product from a company. The customer's decision process is increasingly affected by the MO of the leader of the organization they are buying from.

Maya Enista Smith is the CEO of the Born This Way Foundation, which is documenting youth experiences of mental health challenges and the factors that affect their well-being. The goal is to more effectively leverage resources and ensure all of their programming is grounded in the latest scientific evidence. Smith's favorite saying to live by is "If you are more fortunate than others, it's better to build a longer table than a taller fence." We already have way too many fences and silos in our world. We need to rebuild a whole lot of tables, much longer than any we've had to build before.

Doing versus Being

Being a Rebuilder is not just a way of *doing* things or accomplishing tasks or even building your skill sets. It's just as much a way of *being* (see Figure 7.1). There is no shortage of definitions and descriptions of those two concepts, but maybe the best, and least ethereal one I came across for our purposes is this:

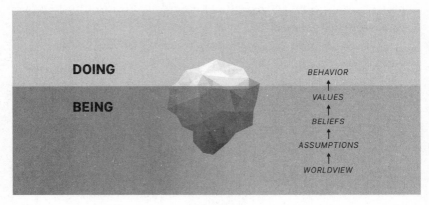

FIGURE 7.1

Doing is what you *do*. It's the actions you take. It's the decisions you make. It's your behavior and all its visible manifestations.

Being is who you *are*. It's what's underneath all of the *doing*. It's your qualities and thought patterns. It's the pattern of beliefs that you hold about yourself and your environment. It's your worldview.[3]

Being a Rebuilder with a Generosity Mindset is absolutely a worldview. It's about the approach to the work, the way you see the variables at play, and the complex equation for finding solutions. Each of the Rebuilders we've looked at operates from a set of values and beliefs and worldview; it's part of what sets them apart and makes them the right leaders for the 2020s.

Just to put an exclamation point on something. There is less and less of that kind of mindset in our world and it's debilitating to civil society. Those leaders who possess that vital trait will be near-unicorns pretty soon, and we will need every one of them we can possibly find to truly address our five megachallenges in the 2020s.

On the Ground

Some of these leaders think at a system level, trying to figure out the root cause, influencing public policy, and working across sectors to solve these intractable problems. Others, like Herb Virgo, who created the Keney Park Sustainability Project (KPSP)[4] site in Hartford, Connecticut, teach composting, gardening, aquaponics,  and hydroponics with a goal of connecting people to the healing power of nature. An *in*-the-ground leader, if you will. Both types of leaders need each other.

Virgo's passion for sustainability has a wonderful origin story. His grandmother loved her rose bushes, and when Virgo was young, he loved to take care of her yard and "see my grandmother's reaction."

Herb Virgo

There was an emergent Generosity Mindset from the time he was a little boy.

That's why Rosanne Haggerty connected me to Virgo as an exemplar. It doesn't take a lot of time with an on-the-ground leader like him (and Debbie Little) to know why Haggerty sees him as vital to the whole solution. He and KPSP are key partners in Community Solutions' population change work in the North End of Hartford. Hopefully, they will be one of the next communities to end chronic homelessness.

As Haggerty explains, "Herb's is the type of organization demonstrating how to build a system approach to community development. He's been open to marrying that with a data-driven, outcomes approach to population-level change. He's the type of leader who will have an outsize role because he's a natural systems thinker who operates in an integrative way."

Virgo is another example of why we need to rebuild more than we need to invent a new wheel. My twenty-plus years in the nonprofit and social sectors has slowly, but surely, shown me that there are very effective leaders already in communities, on the ground. We need to invest and then reinvest in the Herb Virgos within our communities, not invent new programs again and again.

His team at KPSP provides an opportunity for local families in the neighborhood to grow their own food on-site. "That empowerment to be able to grow your own food has been something that we have been amazed at. If you give them the power to feed themselves, you change their lives . . . you change everything. And that's what we're trying to do," he says. KPSP has preserved a 693-acre urban forest by providing individuals employable landscaping and forest management skills and, as a result, it is also creating the next generation of environmental stewards.

People that think that way, so holistically and so openly, with the finite resources he has are the ones that create a whole that is greater than the sum of the parts. He doesn't know how to play a zero-sum game. He knows that the best way to increase his slice is to grow the whole pie and not to figure out how to grow his share at the expense of others. That may have a nice-guy ring to it, but it's far more strategic than it is polite. Actually, Virgo's mind thinks at a system level, too; not "just" one citizen at a time. His vision is to show other communities how to replicate KPSP's work in their cities and states. He thinks expansively and generously.

The Other Howard

One vital dynamic about leadership in the decade ahead is that leaders can show up in so many different ways and places than we are used to seeing. Not only is our world more distributed, but the complexity of our problems is so great that we need a breadth and depth of leaders like never before. Howard Behar, like many of his generation, and today's, found part of his early grounding in leadership theory from Robert Greenleaf's work on servant leadership.[5] One of his comments when I was talking to him about leadership was that it

Howard Behar

takes a "generous mindset."

Behar is a cofounder of Starbucks and a huge believer in how you show up at work should be the same as you show up in every part of your life. I think that's called 24-7 Authenticity, too. When I asked him how generosity shows up in a growing, entrepreneurial company like Starbucks in the 1980s, 1990s, and first decade of the 2000s,

he didn't hesitate: "Success comes from working with people, not on the backs of your people." He said he always knew his people "had to get more out of working than just making money." His job was to serve his people. In many ways, he was ahead of his time.

In the process, of course, he helped create not only a global brand but also one of the first global companies to truly take corporate social responsibility seriously by calling for values-based leadership, revitalizing neighborhoods with unique stores, and investing in the college education of their baristas.

One of the challenges of leading in today's world is how certain qualities like a Generosity Mindset are still able to show up and shine through. It needs to be modeled more in real time real-time to become evident. The other traits are a little more tangible or skills-based; they are more obvious. In Behar's mind, a generous mindset is even more important in today's world, especially right now when so much of how we relate to each other is via a screen.

Having knowing Behar for more than ten years, I have to say he has one inherent asset that he brings to his leadership. He is a naturally generous person. It comes through in how he talks, how he relates to each person. I don't know if that was learned over the last fifty years or if that's just the way he was born, but he is authentically generous. I can't think of a single person I've ever known who has more people call him their best mentor than Howard Behar.

The Downside of a Generosity Mindset

There are two main downsides. First, you'll be balancing competing interests and agendas all the time. You'll get consistently frustrated and you'll need to constantly model generosity. A thick skin plus resilience is the "prescription" for the downside for many of these traits, especially a Generosity Mindset. Working persistently with an open mind to find common ground where it is hard to find definitely puts you in a position of more potential frustration.

Second, a Generosity Mindset requires an adaptive mindset as well. Cecilia Gutierrez said she has to be constantly adapting to other people's languages and approaches; she has to be chameleon-like. Early on in her career, she'd sometimes get lost in the midst of that constant adaptiveness. It can be draining, and the kind of people who are exemplars can often ask more of themselves and not enough of others. At some point, a person's tank can hit empty. You have to find ways to keep your tank fueled.

I'm the Bridge

She is known as "the connector." She is the Bridge Home project manager for Mayor Eric Garcetti of Los Angeles. She manages *relationships* with fifteen offices, managers, and partners *across* the city, nonprofit community, and county. Apryle Brodie is a living metaphor for the Generosity Mindset in everything that she is and does.

As we've explored extensively, our nation is increasingly full of challenges that are hypercomplex and cross-sector. Not only do we need

Apryle Brodie

more Apryle Brodies and her Generosity Mindset, we frankly don't have a *chance* without more and more leaders like her.

The complexity Brodie is dealing with, and her capacity for it, is mind boggling. Her role, by design, is not intended to go deep on one thing; it's to cut across a wide breadth of departments, constituents, and resources. And doing so in a city and county like Los Angeles is about as complex as it gets. And yet, listen to how Brodie goes about her work as a leader, as a Rebuilder. In her words:

- ▶ The right thing happens when people are connected, period.
- ▶ Across my whole life, it's about offering myself and what can I do for others.
- ▶ I'm always searching for what each person needs to get out of it.
- ▶ I always give grace when it's needed.

Maybe most core to her work as a leader is always looking for relationships that can be transformational, not transactional. There is clearly an inspiring element to how she works, but underneath it is a deeply sophisticated mindset. She is playing the real-time game in all of her interactions with people, but she also plays the long game, looking for the transformational. Brodie said that she is always recognizing and discerning those moments and decision points when the whole becomes less than the sum of the parts.

More than any of the vital traits, a Generosity Mindset requires a leader to work at both strategic and tactical levels. It's a pretty high bar of personal and professional competencies. In Brodie's work and beliefs, you can clearly see the very human, real-time way she works. It's the everyday glue that makes complex problems solvable. It's why they call her "the connector." These Rebuilders also need to think strategically, toward what end all these parts are connected, and about the pathway to effectiveness. It's got some of that Complexity Capacity we've talked about and reminds us again how those two traits often coexist.

There is an amusing anecdote to finish Brodie's story. She exudes generosity as much as any of the exemplars of this trait. My initial conversation with her was in the heart of the pandemic, and she was in the closet at her apartment. She shares the place with her sister, so they trade off who does calls in what places when they have business at the same time. If she can exude generosity when she is stuck in a small closet in an apartment in LA, I can only imagine the effect she has in an open room with a wide range of people and no coat hangers or shoe racks cramping her space.

Seven Things We Know about the Generosity Mindset in Leaders for the Future

1. They don't play a zero-sum game. Never have and never will, for any reason.
2. Not always but often, that open, connecting, always-looking-for-what's-next mindset shows up earlier in life experiences.
3. They have value themselves, but the role modeling and culture setting they create can be just as powerful long term.
4. They don't hesitate about or moderate their generosity. This trait is sort of an on-off switch, not a dimmer switch. You could say 24-7 generosity is either fully turned on or not, too.

5. They are constantly figuring out what makes others tick, what will engage them; they are outward focused.

6. Their generosity does not equate with loose or easy-going, in terms of impact and outcomes; often the contrary.

7. This trait often coexists with Complexity Capacity, either in the same person (somewhat rare) or amongst team members (much more common and achievable).

I am a huge admirer of FDR's. He believed in the greatness and generosity of Americans, but was also a cold-blooded politician.

—JON MEACHAM

CHAPTER EIGHT

Data Conviction

W hen there is slowing, more unequal, less certain progress across a broad array of social, health, and economic indicators (megachallenge #4), data becomes an indispensable element in trying to forge a path toward more equal progress across American civil society. With the data, progress is not assured. Without the data, progress is just about impossible.

Think constant learning and improvement. Instead of data being an afterthought to understand social or community impact at a point in time, it's more powerful to develop a relentless focus on understanding the real-world, real-time, ongoing impact of programs, practices, and policies. And ensure that the data being used is the right, not just readily available, data. It can then inform persistent, day-to-day improvement in companies and communities.

And remember that Data Conviction risks being dehumanizing or too formulaic without the humanizing quality of 24-7 Authenticity.

A PILE IS THE vertical support structure used to hold up a bridge. A pile is hammered into the soil beneath the bridge until it reaches the hard sublayer of compacted soil or rock below. Piles leverage the grip and friction of the soil surrounding it to support part of the load of the bridge deck. They have to be as solid as the rock they reach down to. Just like the data we use for economic, health, and social change. It isn't the only part of the "bridge" we are building for America's future, but the data has to be solid because so much rests on top of it. If it's weak or loose, so much can fall apart.

I never guess. It is a capital mistake to theorize before one has data. Insensibly one begins to twist facts to suit theories, instead of theories to suit facts.
—SHERLOCK HOLMES

A Flashlight Instead of a Hammer

Jeff Edmondson's data story starts halfway around the world in an unexcepted place. Gabon is a small western Central African nation, bordered by Republic of the Congo, Cameroon, and the Atlantic

Ocean. It doesn't get any more idealistic than being a Peace Corps volunteer in a remote part of the world. Edmondson set off for Gabon in the spring of 1996 for his two-year stint.

He ended up staying for an extra eighteen months, with another colleague, to serve in the role of regional Peace Corps volunteer to try (and try and try) to transition the

Jeff Edmondson

program from fish farming to animal husbandry. Fish farming was a successful endeavor in the neighboring Congo, so of course it would work the same in Gabon, right? Exactly like things that work in Boise will work just the same in Los Angeles, right?

There was just one problem. Every rainy season in Gabon, the fish farms would get flooded out. Unsure why no one had spoken up before, Edmondson stayed on beyond his normal two-year stint to try to convince the Peace Corps that fish farming was wrong. His message was falling on deaf ears until he brought real data to headquarters, and they finally believed the data and changed course. Edmondson has a relentless, persistent quality about him. The data finally cut through the dissonance. He would return to that lesson many times in his career.

Seven years later, Edmondson was back home in Cincinnati. In 2006, a group of local leaders came together to discuss a new approach to community-wide support for the youth in the region. After much discussion, one of the participants, a county coroner, stood up and said, "As long as we remain program rich and systems poor, we will not get more kids into college. And what's more, I'm going to keep seeing dead kids on my table."

Soon, Edmondson found himself at the center of a new effort across the greater Cincinnati and Northern Kentucky area to build a partnership to support the success of every child—a novel approach involving the private, public, and nonprofit sectors. The underlying belief in cities like Cincinnati, who want to make lasting positive change, is that we can't solve big problems anymore without true cross-sector collaboration. They were right. So the obvious way to start was to try to get actors in the community from Procter & Gamble to the City Recreation Commission to the Endzone Club to the urban public school systems to align according to the different programs being delivered across the community. That was wrong.

All the good intentions of everyone at the table were going in circles. Finally, the head of the United Way at that time said, "We all

assume we understand education the same way, but we may not."
Everyone needed to align for specific outcomes, that is, *data* instead
of *programs*. Once they collectively focused on the data, chaos tuned
into alignment. Different community actors aligned to each data
point, or outcome, and now had a common endgame and language
they could use. Each of them could much more clearly see themselves in the specific solution to a part of the whole challenge. The
data finally cut through the noise.

In both those cases, Edmondson told me (borrowing a line from
Aimee Guidera, founder of the Data Quality Campaign) that the
data was, at first, being "used as a hammer instead of a flashlight."
Data can sometimes be an elusive and improperly used guide for
work in the social sector. Some funders and public entities use data
for retrospective compliance and oversight as opposed to using the
data prospectively to inform where a program is going and what can
be made better; hence the hammer versus the flashlight.

In both those cases, Edmondson was eventually able to get everyone involved to use a flashlight. Believe me, the nonprofit sector,
more than any, needs data flashlights. It's the nature of what they
do, as I've said before, because their outcomes will never be as clear
as earnings per share.

Eventually, Edmondson became the first executive director of the
Strive Partnership of Cincinnati and Northern Kentucky, one of the
most ambitious and, over time, effective community-wide social
change efforts in America. His successor at StriveTogether, the national network, was Complexity Capacity leader Jennifer Blatz. Today, Edmondson is the executive director of community mobilization
at Ballmer Group. In part he is trying to take what he did at Strive-
Together and broaden that Data Conviction and community impact.

Edmondson still remembers one comment in the early days from
John Pepper, then CEO of Procter & Gamble. Pepper told him, "Everyone thinks P&G has perfect data. We don't. We have a lot of data
that is good enough to make better decisions." That's what global

companies like P&G make a lot of decisions based upon. It soon became Edmondson's charter to convince everyone that data (1) really matters and (2) doesn't have to be perfect.

StriveTogether and its impact data is telling us that real change in communities is possible. Same goes for Rosanne Haggerty's work on homelessness, Michael McAfee's work on Promise Neighborhoods, and a few others. They are run by people with huge hearts and brains who care about changing the world and are guided by a never-ending commitment to data.

It's doesn't have to be perfect data; it needs to be good enough data. But without data, positive, real change in communities is barely possible. Remember Sondra Samuels, who said simply, "My organization doesn't exist without data." You'll know one of these "data-convicted" leaders distinctly when the topic of data comes up. People like Edmondson are excited, animated, and energized as if they were talking about their firstborn (well, almost). That excitement is driven by how much positive power real, shared data can have in helping teams, communities, and companies get out of silos and find common ground to work together.

A Definition of Data Conviction

Data Conviction may seem a little dry or stale as a vital leadership trait, but it's not. It's the conviction about and passion for data that is an absolutely necessary mindset for Rebuilders in the 2020s. Think about how complex the challenges are that our private, public, and non-profit sectors are going to face in a post-COVID world. Without data to create some baseline degree of clarity, as well as a basis for bringing competing worldviews together, there is little chance for success.

Let's define this as not just understanding but being able to process and then get good at interpreting and using data. This is about a core belief that the data is an indispensable part of the answer, that data is not just a tactic or a number; it's strategic. We know that good programs are necessary, but without the data, they are not sufficient.

The two biggest differences between the private versus nonprofit and public sectors are (1) the private sector has one primary bottom line, net profit, whereas nonprofit and public sectors have many and much less black-and-white outcomes; and (2) in the private sector the customer pays for the product, whereas in the nonprofit and public sectors payment often comes through third parties. A primary function of data for social change is trying to find the best replacement, or create effective proxies, for a bottom line and paying customer. It isn't perfect, but it is way, way better than the absence of it. As we've said before, data is vital, but usually not sufficient. The absence of data is crippling.

Does It Get Any Tougher Than Philly?

Bi Vuong currently lives in New York after previous stops in DC, Philly, and Boston. Her personality is a great roll-up of those four cities—strong, savvy, and fearless. She is the kind of person it took to be a part of a critical restructuring of Philadelphia schools in 2013–14. Her work in this restructuring is a perfect example of

someone with a deep understanding of data and a true commitment to evidence while using that understanding and commitment to do right. In this case, for the students and families of Philadelphia facing a tough situation.

Several years ago, the School District of Philadelphia faced a shortfall of hundreds of millions of dollars, in part due to losing

Bi Vuong

tens of thousands of students in the first decade of the century. The math said there was no choice: there would have to be closings, restructurings, and consolidation. Alongside the demands of all that ugly math were real families with real kids who were deeply connected to their neighborhood schools. They wanted their kids to get a great education.

Dr. William Hite, still the superintendent there today, was the driving force of the restructuring work. He used data to inform his decisions and make the changes possible (I could write about him in 24-7 Authenticity). Vuong played a key role behind the scenes as the director of the Strategy Delivery Unit in the Office of the Superintendent, and eventually the district's deputy CFO, by providing him with this necessary data.

When any district is trying to make decisions of that significance, it can fall apart if the data isn't real or the leadership isn't authentic. Vuong was a key part of the team trying to be as transparent as possible about sharing data with the citizens of Philly. In Vuong's words, they put "every single data point online." That's a powerful statement on its own. That's making the data itself 24-7 authentic.

They looked at student-level data, facility utilization, enrollment, financial projections, academic performance, and on and on. And when that data and their best thinking informed a set of recommendations, they took those recommendations to the people around town who would be directly affected. They got as granular as needed, for example, showing citizens the average distance from their current school to a proposed new school. Data in real terms for people's daily lives.

The data also told the community that the district did its work and took their findings very seriously. The data was informative on its own, but it also told a story about how thorough and committed the district had been in their diligence. They listened to the community and revised again and again. If a citizen had a proposal, the district invited them to work with them and revisited their recommendation. Over time, the district made numerous changes concerning which schools to recommend for closure and the new school configuration.

Not everyone was okay with the final decisions, but most people understood what was behind the decisions. The School District of Philadelphia fought the hard battle back to financial solvency. As we see time and again, the data gives a hard, subjective, challenging goal a chance for people to get into alignment around goals. Today, Vuong is the head of the education practice at Project Evident,[1] using many of the same principles about data to work with more and more school districts, and education nonprofits, around the United States.

Is There an Approach to Data That Matters?

Or is it just a function of a few unicorns like the people in this book? Data, in and of itself, is nothing. Data needs to be imbued with analysis, interpretation, values . . . and authenticity. In a world of social impact, where there isn't just one bottom line, what does good, strong data look like and how do we access it? Here's a simple working definition that can be used for more effective decision-making: data plus analysis equals evidence.

If you hang out around people like the thirty-eight Rebuilders in this book long enough, patterns emerge. There is a methodology for using data for effective community change, and it can be shared and replicated. But it's not easy. Let me share a handful of principles for data that make a real difference:

> ▶ No data stands on its own. There is always context, there are disparities, which is part of why these leaders are so key. They know how to navigate the numbers. It's often a danger to look at impact data in isolation. You have to be willing to disaggregate by race, class, gender, and other demographic characteristics that matter in your community. Data is the

starting point for this work and then needs to be used to drive honesty, transparency, and accountability all along the way.

▶ Make it continuous, real-time, and dynamic. Data that matters is not done once a year or at one moment in time. Think of the revolution in sports data and analytics. Sports teams now use data to constantly change what they are doing, and they use it as real-time as the rules will allow. In the NFL, quarterbacks are looking at data on the sidelines during the whole game. Practitioners at nonprofits need to have the same real-time ownership of and facility with program data, instead of how it's been in the past.

▶ Data needs to live on the front lines. It needs to be owned by the practitioners driving and delivering and interpreting the programs. The social worker on the street, the head of evaluation at a social change organization, the garbage truck driver in Phoenix, Arizona. Put the data in their hands, not at some third-party research firm that has much less connection to or sense of urgency about the real-time work in communities.

▶ Bring stakeholders together. There are a whole lot of people who will care if you've got good data. But if there isn't buy-in, it won't matter. Bring people from across organizations that share this Data Conviction to interpret it, determine its implications, and align on actions going forward. That's what Jeff Edmondson started with StriveTogether and Jennifer Blatz is expanding even further.

▶ Identify mileposts along the journey. Be as clear as you can about tangible progress along the journey, the contributing indicators related to an ultimate outcome (for example, attendance rates related to early grade reading). Publish those trendlines and goals. Again, think about Edmondson and Strive and what John Pepper at P&G told him. I tell my friends that nonprofits use data the same way for-profit businesses do eighty-nine out of ninety days. Nonprofits don't have that fencepost of quarterly earnings, but the other eighty-nine days of data was much the same; we looked for signals, dashboards, indicators that told us our work was going in the right direction. Or not.

▶ There has to be co-ownership and co-creation. Shared buy-in and belief about the data needs to be built through ongoing, authentic community engagement. This is not optional. We no longer do community and corporate social responsibility work *to* a community; we do it *with* them. That may seem obvious now, but it's a real sea change. The people involved have to be demographically, racially, and ethnically representative. The long-term difference in doing so can be transformational.

If you want to study an organization that is trying to help the whole sector get data and evidence right, check out Bi Vuong's work at Project Evident (PE).[2] PE was created out of a deep dissatisfaction with the current approaches to data and evidence in communities. The goal is to build a healthier system for evidence that will benefit all stakeholders and, most importantly, the greater good. PE is focused squarely on many of the approaches above—changing from compliance- to community-driven data, from static to continuous evidence, and from data being owned by third parties to being owned by the people on the front lines doing the real work.

If you want to study a project that is getting data right, check out Community Solutions' Built for Zero. If you want to accuse me of being the head of the Rosanne Haggerty fan club, I'll plead guilty. Their strategies are about community-level measurement that looks at the total number of specific individuals experiencing homelessness. Communities rapidly test new ideas and understand if those efforts are working.

They use comprehensive, real-time, by-name data so they know everyone experiencing homelessness by name, in real time. Billy Beane, who helped revolutionize baseball and whose story was told in *Money Ball*, would be proud of and admire their work.[3]

Cutting across Lines

Many of our data stories have been about how it's not just the numbers. Nicollette Staton's story is about *how* that Data Conviction is put into play effectively. It's one thing to have the data and numbers, but it's another to know how to use it to lead across departments and colleagues. Staton uses data horizontally.

Nicollette Staton

She is the CPO for the City of Cincinnati. The chief performance officer, that is. She starts from a core idea that "data empowers leaders." We know that not every municipal leader believes that . . . yet. In 24-7 Authenticity, we talked about the idea that you *need* to be authentic and transparent before you *have* to be. The same is true for data.

Let's be clear: people in leadership positions who don't believe in data, don't have a strong conviction, and aren't willing to be 100 percent transparent about the data (good or bad) are not real leaders for the 2020s. They fear the truth in the data. That description does not fit Staton. She is a young leader, an emerging Rebuilder.

She has a strategy for broadening the Data Conviction across an organization. The ultimate goal is broad adoption and buy-in, which isn't going to happen overnight. In Staton's case, that's across twenty-six departments at the City of Cincinnati. She is inserting her work and the city's data into every silo. It's about building trust across and ultimately breaking down silos.

The City of Cincinnati is no different than other major municipal governments (see Los Angeles, Andy Lipkis and Apryle Brodie). There are lots of departments focused on their real-time, day-to-day work; they have to be. Data and leaders like Staton can be the glue that ties the good work together. But it takes a deep conviction, because it isn't easy in any city.

Staton and her team are dedicated full-time to championing data and performance management. One of the office's keys to success here is the wraparound support provided through internal data consulting for departments and leveraging the innovation arm of the office not only to help departments create data systems but to develop policies and practices that help them reach the data-driven outcomes that they commit to.

Start with the simpler, less interpretative data. Build trust. Move on to the more complex and interpretative data. Build trust. Over time, show how data can empower them to be leaders. Build trust. As much as anyone I talked to, Staton's story had this cyclical, reinforcing dynamic of trust building with data, which then builds on itself and eventually creates critical mass and changes a whole culture.

Cincinnati has a robust enterprise data warehouse that is connected to more than two hundred data sources across the city, so the scope of the work can proceed only at the speed of trust. When does that trust-built-on-data matter most? When a crisis hits. On March 13, 2020, Cincinnati suspended Staton's team's regular operations and redeployed their skill sets and relationships built over the past five years to support the city's response to the public health pandemic. Governor DeWine, at the state level, was one of the early, exemplary leaders. He didn't politicize it; he let the data inform his decisions, and I suspect that clarified the response required of every city across the state, including Cincinnati.

The groundwork Cincinnati had done not only internally but with its external partners had primed leaders in key positions to lean on data and processes to respond to an unprecedented emergency. Leaders with true Data Conviction don't just build a stronger organization for the "normal" times, whenever that last was. They also make organizations more resilient and prepared when the crises hit. No one knows what the decade ahead holds, but we know it won't be normal. We do know the future will need people with a shared conviction about the data. Leaders like Nicollette Staton, who know how to translate that data into trust.

The Downside of Data Conviction

Data can be awesome, except (1) you need to get it right—yes, you can make mistakes, but not too many or too often; (2) there is a lot of dis- and misinformation out there, as we well know, so it is a constant challenge to make sure data is commonly understood; and (3) once you start down the data-driven path, there is no going back. Simple statements, but not simple to live and practice for the long term. The potential downsides of Data Conviction seem most obvious of any of the five traits so we won't belabor this point just to fill space on the page.

Helping People Like Felipe Thrive

Jennifer Park is one of those people you meet and think she can probably do just about anything and do it really well. She is the Director of Certification and Community for What Works Cities. They help local governments improve residents' lives by using data and evidence to tackle pressing challenges. The important part of her  story isn't the data she works with. It's how she uses, and helps others use, data to help them be better leaders.

I'm not arguing that data didn't matter in the past; it has for a long time. It's about how data has become an increasingly important tool of leadership. That will only increase further in the years ahead.

Jennifer Park

Park has a unique wide-angle view because she sees data in use across cities and city leadership all over America. Here are some of the most important ways she sees data used to lead:

▸ Data creates alignment. Data provides everyone the opportunity, up and down the organization, to make informed decisions.

▸ Data empowers failure. With the data, you can show how you tried, how you failed, and how you can try again so much more effectively than you can without the data.

▸ Data facilitates disaggregation. Doing so gets the data to a usable level where far better decisions can be made and poor decisions can be exposed more easily.

▸ Data enables engagement. Data allows citizens to engage better and in a more tangible way with the decisions leaders make (see Bi Vuong and Philly school district).

Park made one more great point. The support for data in the culture of a public entity needs to come from both the top and the bottom rungs of the organization. From the mayor to the data analyst. At the end of the day, the primary thing data can do is make real change happen in communities. To date, thirteen cities have reached gold or silver certification from Jennifer's organization, What Works Cities, a recognition that they have the right people, processes, and policies in place to put data and evidence at the center of decision-making.

Think about a data dashboard like this in a city like Los Angeles, partnered with a strategy like Community Solutions. These kinds of data and leaders, like Jenn Park and Rosanne Haggerty, are coming together; they are converging. It takes time, and someday it's going to make a big damn difference.

Park and Haggerty have helped dozens of cities begin to more actively own and use their data, and the cumulative effect of all of that municipal work is constantly raising the bar on the quality, transparency, and usability of data for American cities. That's a big deal and will get bigger.

For cities to make real progress on intractable problems, they will, by definition, have to be more willing to fail—both inside the organization and outside with the community. For mayors and city managers who have courage and commitment and authenticity, data can empower them to take smart risks—the kind true leaders like our Rebuilders have to take for our communities in the years ahead. Rebuilders like Jenn Park will be the kind of leader who empowers all of those other leaders.

Eight Things about Data Conviction in Our Leaders for the Future

1. Once you start into the world of open and transparent data, you have to keep going. There is no turning back. Don't start unless you are ready and committed.
2. The data will always be iterative, rarely static. Make sure everyone knows that and build that into the culture.
3. Don't let *great* be the enemy of *good*.

4. The numbers on their own usually aren't enough. Stories need data to back them up. You need both; you need to be good at telling data stories.

5. You have to think of data as strategic, as a leadership asset, not just an important tactic or number.

6. You need community buy-in on the data. Being as transparent as you can increases the collective ownership and buy-in.

7. Be sure ownership and support of the data come from both the top down and the bottom up.

8. Data Conviction is often paired with and mutually reinforces 24-7 Authenticity.

Any enterprise CEO really ought to be able to ask a question that involves connecting data across the organization, be able to run a company effectively, and especially to be able to respond to unexpected events. Most organizations are missing this ability to connect all the data together.
                                            —TIM BERNERS-LEE,
                                            founder of the internet

CHAPTER NINE

Cross-Sector Fluency

When the lines between and the historical norms of our private, nonprofit, and public sectors are intersecting and overlapping as never before (megachallenge #5), Cross-Sector Fluency becomes a must-have, not a nice-to-have. I don't mean sort of hopping into a project in another sector and then going back into your longtime professional sector silo for most of your career. I mean genuine immersion in the other two sectors or at least one of the other two sectors.

To be clear, lack of Cross-Sector Fluency is not a judgment of one's inadequacy, personally or professionally. I am simply articulating a vital trait leaders need to have for the future.

Cross-Sector Fluency often provides the glue that brings everything else together. Not just because of the experience itself but because it suggests that those who have it view the world more holistically, are more willing to see the nuance, have a wider lens, make trade-offs, and create the whole solution. They aren't unicorns, but they're pretty invaluable.

A BRIDGE BEARING provides a resting surface between the bridge's piers and its deck, connecting the foundation to the substructure. Its purpose is to allow controlled movement between the two surfaces. Pound for pound, it is the most critical element in a whole bridge structure, one that allows the different forces to have the flexibility and give-and-take to stay in balance. In the same way, someone with Cross-Sector Fluency can often allow the different players some flexibility, facilitate give-and-take, and help bring the systems and people together and keep them in balance.

When I was a kid, there was no collaboration. It was you with a camera bossing your friends around. But as an adult, filmmaking is all about appreciating the talents of the people you surround yourself with and knowing you could never have made any of these films by yourself.   —STEVEN SPIELBERG

Finding a Two-Way Value Proposition

As I sat in a Seattle conference room in mid-2019 and listened to Michelle Nunn talk about her work over the previous three years, her story pivoted effortlessly across all three sectors of American civil society—private, public, and nonprofit. Nunn is the CEO of CARE USA, the American member of CARE International, the humanitarian aid and development agency. She talked about just getting back from several weeks in the Middle East, where she visited refugee camps across Syria and Jordan. She was working to better understand how CARE USA could provide aid in the midst of a massive crisis (this was a pre-COVID massive crisis).

Michelle Nunn

She weaved in a story about her work with the executive leadership of PepsiCo and how their supply chain and corporate knowledge are a significant asset for CARE. Just as naturally, she referenced her interactions with USAID, explaining how government sector aid dollars flow to support refugees and eliminate gender- and race-based violence. All of that on the heels of a strong run as a candidate for the US Senate in 2014. That kind of native fluency across all three sectors is the new kind of leadership our world needs and demands as we move further into the 2020s.

When I talked to Nunn more about her work, I was curious about how she learned to work the way she does today. How are people like her, and everyone else in this section on Cross-Sector Fluency, playing the kind of roles she is? She shared another story about a corporate giant, Cargill.

There has been a fifty-plus-year partnership between Cargill and CARE. Back in the '60s and '70s, it was a stay-in-your-silos relationship. Cargill bought lots of CARE packages to send around the world. Useful, clean, and simple. Today, Nunn explained, CARE's relationship with Cargill is multidimensional, one example being how Cargill leverages CARE's deep knowledge about the farmers and the communities that make up Cargill's supply chain in West Africa. Cargill leverages CARE.

CARE also leverages Cargill's global knowledge, just like with PepsiCo. Nunn said that if CARE really wants to scale, that is, create more positive impact and less suffering in human lives around the globe, they can't do it without private sector partners like Cargill. In simple terms, each organization has become a strategic business asset of the other. That's a powerful reality in 2020.

One more story. In Africa, CARE wants to help female farmers diversify and increase their income. If you need to better understand the value and power of women earning more income in developing countries, just type those nine words into a Google search.

Mars (M&M's, Snickers, Milky Way, etc.) sources cocoa from West Africa. In fact, 70 percent of all cocoa in the world comes from farms in West Africa. Just like CARE, they are always looking for growth. Mars, and other companies sourcing cocoa, are committed to improving incomes for the farmers that grow cocoa. Why? A robust cocoa supply chain is a necessity.

In working with farmers and building their incomes in a sustained way, Mars looked to CARE and its Village Savings and Loan Association (VSLA) model, which CARE pioneered thirty years ago. Women in small groups of fifteen to twenty-five save their money together and take small, low-interest loans from those savings. Women then invest that money as they see fit—paying school fees, starting side businesses, investing in their farms. Mars believes in CARE's VSLA model so much so that in 2018 the company made a commitment to scale VSLAs across its cocoa supply chain in West Africa. We're used to nonprofits leveraging for-profits. Now we've come full circle.

As Nunn told me, it's good when a for-profit company donates money or volunteers its people. But the real power is when you can align the economic interests of both entities. That's when it becomes absolutely vital to have leaders for the future with Cross-Sector Fluency. Today, CARE is reaching about 7.6 million such people around the world. The problem is they want, no they need, to reach sixty million around the world. We need truly cross-sector, fluent leaders like Nunn *now*.

Twenty years ago, Nunn was the cofounder of Hands On Atlanta, the original group that inspired the Hands On Network of volunteers across America. It merged into Points of Light, which is a global network of volunteer-mobilizing organizations that serve more than 250 cities across thirty-seven countries around the world.

She started learning cross-sector lessons more than twenty years ago, lessons that strongly inform how the CARE stories above have unfolded. It's cool to see how these lessons learned not only come full circle but have an additive, sort of exponential effect to them over time. Cocreating mutually valuable global supply chains with Fortune 500 international companies is the embodiment of Cross-Sector Fluency. The great thing about Nunn is, like many of the Rebuilders in this story, she's just building up momentum. For the sake of America, we better hope so. Can't wait to see her the next time she's in a conference room, real or virtual, talking about what CARE is taking on next.

A Definition of Cross-Sector Fluency

The dictionary definition of *fluency* is helpful: gracefulness and ease of movement or style. Our challenges today do not exist in silos, within one sector or another; they cut across sectors. We've said that enough times. A generation ago, all three sectors were mostly able to live in their own ecosystem, tangentially paying attention to the other two sectors around it. Those days are long gone, but it does point out a tension point. The fact that the three sectors are running together is in contrast to the siloing of America that we've talked about many times, especially in chapter 2.

While individuals are more siloed, solving big challenges will require many leaders to be less siloed and have more Cross-Sector Fluency.

If a private sector company wants to be economically successful, its leaders have to understand how to navigate the public sector as well as the nonprofit sector in the community around them. If a social sector entity is trying to make progress on an intractable social problem, they cannot do it without the public sector if they want to make true, sustained progress. And the private sector is now an asset—human, financial, and intellectual—that is indispensable for tackling the community challenges nonprofits have been working on for decades. All of those interactions are positive dependencies and virtuous feedback loops.

Cultural Translator

Cheryl Dorsey is a natural fit for being the leader of a movement of emerging social entrepreneurs. She is one herself. Even more rele-

Cheryl Dorsey

vant, Dorsey is fluent in cross-sector talk and walk. She was the daughter of parents who were some of the first in their families to attend and graduate from college. She grew up middle class in Baltimore as a black kid in an integrated Jewish neighborhood with a Baptist grandma. She celebrated Hanukkah and Christmas. She went to Harvard Medical School, and her first stop after graduating was in inner-city Boston to work in the neighborhoods of Dorchester, Mattapan, and Roxbury. No wonder Cheryl Dorsey is a self-described "cultural translator."

Especially during college, she was also trying to reconcile the American creed with the white supremacy she saw around her. She studied African American history and shameful incidents like the Tuskegee syphilis study. She wrote her college thesis on public health infrastructure for free black people in pre–Civil War Baltimore. Out of Harvard Medical School, she headed across the subway tracks (same city, but worlds apart) to launch the Family Van, a community-based mobile health unit. So many of these Rebuilders reveal their true, good, authentic, caring selves pretty early in their lives, often right out of college like Dorsey.

About twenty years ago, the term *social entrepreneur* came into vogue. In some ways, social entrepreneur, coined by Bill Drayton at Ashoka,[1] embodies the blurring of the sectors. If Drayton coined the term and started the movement, Cheryl Dorsey, CEO of Echoing

Green for the last ten years, was one of the most important leaders who grew and scaled that movement.

She's worked at the White House and alongside social entrepreneurs as wide-ranging as younger leaders combating desertification in Tunisia with innovative farming practices to designing mobile tools to curb police violence in the United States. She guided the acceleration of a global movement of Echoing Green alumni, alongside Ashoka Fellows, who are truly helping change the world. Alumni like Michelle Obama, Wendy Kopp, Michael Brown, and Billy Shore. Organizations like Global Health Corps, the African Leadership Academy, and One Acre Fund. And that's the tip of the iceberg.

Some leaders acquire a trait through experience, some through schooling. In Dorsey's case, it's a combination. Her upbringing got her ready to play a cross-sector role as much as anything else did. She also has a very cogent point of view about the events in the first year of this new decade.

Her med school background and smarts taught her that epidemics are often moments of significant social as well as health changes. In early 2020, that might well have sounded like an intellectually correct but largely uninteresting discussion. In March 2020 and beyond, it's top of mind for everyone.

In Dorsey's words, this inflection point for America will take us down "either a transformational or a tribalistic path."

Leaders like Dorsey are going to be uniquely valuable in the years ahead because she knows deeply how to sit at the intersection of the conversations among the three sectors. She's spent time in all three, knows all three, can speak to all three. She is supremely accomplished professionally and supremely prepared experientially. To add just a little more texture to Cheryl's story:

Frankly, few of us have an upbringing like hers. She described it to me as a lived experience of "forged trauma." Occasionally the right leaders show up because the path they took in life, intentionally and not, prepares them exceptionally well for an unequal, siloed

America. Her life has been all about living through division and silos. Today, Dorsey is a Rebuilder.

Flying Fish

There are plenty of leaders we've talked about that are strategic
about their leadership. Few of them are any more strategic than
Heather Redman. She is a cofounder of Flying Fish Venture Capital,
named after the famous Seattle fish throwers at Pike Place Market.

They focus on early-stage, Pacific Northwest–based artificial intelligence and machine learning start-ups. She is all about
positive change and being intentional on
how she best leverages herself to meet her
region's and her own goals. She lives and
works at the intersection of the civic, political, and private sectors.

Heather Redman

Perhaps the most strategic part of her ap-
proach is seeing expertise and leadership in one of those domains
as a leg up in the other sectors. You have a vantage point on one
"hill" that lets you more effectively see the other ones. What Redman
knows from the political sector influences how she sees the regional
economy. Her private sector platform enables her to more power-
fully see how vital it is that she actively leads in the civic sector. If
Redman builds influence in one sector, she can leverage it into another sector. That is the very essence of Cross-Sector Fluency. She is
playing chess, not checkers.

There is one more vital intersection of those sectors for Redman.
We talked about artificial intelligence (AI) and machine learning
(ML) way back in the Where We Are chapter about tech as amplifier.
She is a leader that is keenly aware of the potential, awesome and
terrible, of both forms of future tech. That's part of why Redman

and the team picked AI and ML. They know tech can no longer exist in some vacuum or silo on its own, especially when it comes to technology like AI, which will have increasingly profound effects on our world in so many ways, many of which we don't even understand yet. Redman knows it and she is the kind of Rebuilder that will be a steward of all that power for the good.

As we've discussed before, sometimes the early lives of these leaders foreshadowed their future. Redman "grew up in chaos." She was the only child of hippies who grew up on a commune in rural Oregon. She had to learn to navigate a unique system and wide range of people from an early age. She learned that, in order to survive and someday thrive, you have to learn how to get along with just about everyone. If you look at Redman's LinkedIn profile, you have to keep clicking and clicking on her Experiences to get to the full list, as long a list as I've ever seen. When you scan through the breadth and depth of private, nonprofit, and public sector experiences she's had, it reads like the quintessential profile of a leader for the future with abundant Cross-Sector Fluency—and she's not done yet.

Profits versus Purpose

Purpose coming alongside profits in corporate America was more than a ripple before COVID and the tragedy of George Floyd. Now it's a wave and may soon become as powerful and inexorable and constant as the currents that run through the seven seas. There is a sense that capitalism isn't working for everyone or even many people. Some of the people leading the way in that belief that capitalism isn't working the way it should are somewhat unexpected; that is, the CEOs of those same companies leading our less-than-optimal capitalist economy. Our less-than-optimal system is better than just about any other economic system out there globally, but it's not working the way we need it to.

Governments in this world right now have a little bit of a hard time, and global governance is broken. Populism, xenophobia, nationalism . . . all these things are going in the wrong direction. Meanwhile these issues are piling up. Cybersecurity, financial markets, climate change . . . coronavirus. These are global issues that need global coordination. I believe it is the duty of the private sector to step up and fill that void and be responsible. We are not elected bodies, but we do have to fill that void. And it's in the interest of business. And increasingly, business understands that. —PAUL POLMAN,

CEO, Unilever

The economic, social, and health dynamics we've talked about are challenges enough. Let's add one more dimension to the increasingly complex context our future leaders must navigate: the rise of stakeholder, not just shareholder, capitalism, i.e., the explicit conversation about purpose and people (their employees, their customers, their communities) being just as important as profits.

There was a seminal statement made in August 2019 by the Business Roundtable.[2] The Roundtable is about as powerful and connected of a network of Fortune 500 CEOs as you will find anywhere in the world. Walmart, General Motors, Apple, Chase Bank, and on and on, though lacking the diversity of leaders you see in this book. Their "Statement on the Purpose of a Corporation" is critical for our purposes. I pulled out a handful of key, relevant statements:

Americans deserve an economy that allows each person to succeed through hard work and creativity and to lead a life of meaning and dignity. . . .

While each of our individual companies serves its own corporate purpose, we share a fundamental commitment to all of our stakeholders. We commit to:

▶ Delivering value to our customers . . .

- ▶ Investing in our employees. This starts with compensating them fairly and providing important benefits. . . . We foster diversity and inclusion, dignity, and respect.
- ▶ Dealing fairly and ethically with our suppliers. We are dedicated to serving as good partners to the other companies, large and small, that help us meet our missions.
- ▶ Supporting the communities in which we work. We respect the people in our communities and protect the environment by embracing sustainable practices across our businesses.
- ▶ Generating long-term value for shareholders. . . . We are committed to transparency and effective engagement with shareholders.

Each of our stakeholders is essential. We commit to deliver value to all of them, for the future success of our companies, our communities, and our country.

There it is in living color for all the world to see. And for them to be accountable for. It won't be enough only to maximize profit. Leaders need to make sure their organizations help the communities around them. Is this private sector statement for real? Skepticism is valid and only time and action, not words, will tell.

Alan Murray, CEO of Fortune.com, remarked that, "Having covered business as a journalist for four decades, I firmly believe something different is going on today. In the way the best CEOs think and talk about their responsibilities to society. The current pandemic is likely to widen the rifts that have plagued Western society in recent years. Between knowledge workers and manual workers, the well-educated and the less well-educated, top-tier cities, and the rest. Businesses will need to play a bigger role in healing those rifts or risk losing their operating licenses in the eyes of their stakeholders."

There is a potentially even more powerful point. It's not just reducing the negative impacts, it's about how much of a positive difference this could make in addressing our foundational economic, social, and health challenges discussed in Part II. The private sector has financial and human resources that the nonprofit and public sectors can't and never will match. It is two-thirds of the American economy.

Most of those resources will always be directed toward bottom-line net profit. But if we even think about 5 percent more of American capitalist resources truly attuned (not always totally dedicated) to the purpose statement above, it will matter. And not a little bit.

All three sectors of American society are undergoing significant transformations during the same time we have become a more unequal, siloed nation. The lines between them are blurring; you can't just stay in your lane anymore. The private sector, either by proactive choice or reactive reality, has to deal with a lot more than just one bottom line and a homogeneous group of shareholders and investors. In the blurring of the three sectors are great opportunities for big progress if we have the kinds of leaders who can navigate, leaders with Cross-Sector Fluency.

Maybe one of the most significant remarks I've seen in the last year came from Intel CEO Bob Swan. He recently created an ambitious set of targets for his company and his industry to reduce greenhouse gas emissions, transition to green power, restore clean water to local communities, eliminate landfill waste, combat human rights abuses in the supply chain, and double the number of women and minorities in leadership positions.

Referring to why he was ramping up these social goals, he said, "We said let's make sure we are using our purpose as a screen for how we attack these problems. It is not 'How is our product going to be the best?' but rather 'How do we make sure we enrich lives on earth?'"[3]

Those are big words from a very big, highly respected, influential private sector company. Ten years ago, I would have been sure that statement was made by a nonprofit executive director or a mayor. Five years ago, it might have been said by a corporate CEO, but I'm not sure if I would have believed it. Today, I'm hopeful in no small part because of the kinds of leaders with Cross-Sector Fluency you are reading about and learning from here. Corporate leaders like Swan need, and will ultimately fail without, Rebuilders.

Two more statements from decades-long business-minded leaders to close off this discussion. First from Mark Kramer, Founder of FSG:

> The idea that global companies can take a leading role in social progress is not wrong; the question is how they can do so in a way that realistically achieves social impact and delivers value to their shareholders. High-level global partnerships . . . rarely actually solve problems. These initiatives collapse under their own weight.
>
> The only way to avoid this fate is for a company to have a clear strategy about when, where, and how to develop highly targeted coalitions that advance progress on the specific issues and in the particular regions that connect most closely to their business. [4]

My translation: local solutions are essential to tackling global problems.Rebuilders are essential to tackling problems.

Maybe even more profoundly, from Michael Porter of HBS legendary fame for *Competitive Strategy*:

> Actually, business profits from solving from social problems. That's where the real profit comes. Let's take pollution. We've learned that actually reducing pollution and emissions is generating profit. It saves money. It makes the business more productive. It doesn't waste resources. . . . Issue by issue by issue, we start to learn that there's no trade-off between social progress and economic efficiency in any fundamental sense.

Another issue is health. What we've found is the health of employees is something business should treasure, because that health allows those employees to be more productive and come to work and not be absent. The deeper work, the new work, the new thinking on the interface between business and social problems is actually showing that there's a fundamental, deep synergy.

Full Alignment

I was emailing Suzi Sosa for some advice and feedback as I was writing this book. In the midst of talking to her about Cross-Sector Fluency,

Suzi Sosa

she added a P.S. to one email: "I did my grad work at the Kennedy School, then went to serve in the US Dept of Commerce, my first day of work was Sept. 10, 2001. Then into the start-up world. Then started multiple nonprofits, then went to academia, and then started a social enterprise. There is a lot to be gained from having first-person experience in each of these worlds vs. dismissing 'corporations,' 'nonprofits,' or 'government' as being inept without ever having experienced it yourself." I thought, maybe I shouldn't get her advice *about* the book, maybe Sosa should be *in* the book.

Her journey has brought her to a place of professional clarity that enables her to be truly fluent in just about every dimension of Cross-Sector Fluency. The for-profit company she founded a few years ago, Verb, is based on an approach that is common among many of these Rebuilders; that is, creating an enterprise first and foremost as an expression of her values.

Sosa's personal mission is to "help people discover possibilities they weren't able to before, to help wake people up." And Verb, for her, is about people using their learning and development platform to discover that "anything is possible for anyone, including new ways of being in your job and other parts of your life." The alignment is clean and powerful. And good business.

Being values-driven combined with her breadth of experience makes her a perfect cross-sector leader. Her values keep her centered no matter where she is, and her experiences have taught her to view her employees, customers, investors, and the community as stakeholders. She sees her power coming from the collective choices made by those stakeholders, not by any right bestowed upon her because of her title. I've always found Sosa to be exceptionally, unerringly, unavoidably authentic as well.

Patient Impatience

Madge Vasquez has been all over all three sectors, and many of the stops along her professional journey involved two or all three  at the same time. At the global consulting firm Accenture, she focused on public sector clients. At Wachovia Bank, her focus was on community development. Today, she is the CEO of Mission Capital in Austin, Texas, where she brings forward her consulting services and leadership development work from her private sector days to help build stronger nonprofits.

Madge Vasquez

Perhaps her most important stop was a master's in public administration at the Lyndon B. Johnson School of Public Affairs at the University of Texas. She educated herself about policy because of her parents and grandparents, who were all farmworkers. She knew how important policy change was to give people like her family, and herself, opportunities her parents never had. She was the first to go to college in her family and she never forgets that. Everything she does is about paying forward the gift her parents gave her.

When I asked her what she's learned from working across all three sectors so many times, often more than one at the same time, her answer was perfect: "patient impatience." She needs to combine the sense of urgency from her nonprofit work, the speed of her private sector work, and the steady, if slow, progress toward change in the public sector.

Living at the intersection of all three sectors and knowing the ins and outs of each is very natural to Vasquez at this point. She says it's been an "incredible journey that constantly expands her tool kit." Her latest work is on breaking through the systemic barriers to more people of color in leadership. Everything she's done previously in her career seems to run into the next thing she takes on, enabling and empowering her to take on and lead change from any and all angles. Leaders like Vasquez, and her advocacy for more leaders of color, is not just more relevant in 2020, it's vital for the 2020s.

The Downside of Cross-Sector Fluency

Maybe here's the best way to sum it up: it's still somewhat of a "wild west" getting these three sectors to effectively, sustainably interact and blend in with one another. We're still learning by trial and error. Now we're commingling these three huge spheres, and the consequences when things fail in one sector can be felt more deeply since they ripple across all three interconnected sectors. The analogies to the current global pandemic should race to top of mind. The more the sectors connect, the more interdependent they become, in potentially and mostly positive, but also negative ways.

In the past, when there was greater separation, if something got messed up in one sector, at least you had the checks and balances and a sort of safety net from the other two. Now, as the lines blur, when failure or corruption happens for a venture connecting all three at once, the impact is worse. This blurring is, on the whole, a very good dynamic, especially if it's being led by individuals with the Cross-Sector Fluency like we have in these Rebuilders.

At the end of the day, can we make 1+1+1=10, or is it something less than 3 because it's too hard? Cross-sector Rebuilders know how to optimize that equation.

Who Really Wants to Run for Office These Days?

This guy is as cross-sector fluent as they come. To top it off, now he is running for the California State Senate. One of Josh Becker's challenges in running for public office is conveying the value and relevance of his extensive cross-sector experience. Maybe not surprisingly, some people that have spent most of their careers in one sector don't always see the value proposition of Cross-Sector Fluency.

Josh Becker

On the campaign trail in 2020, he found his voice in a crowded field of candidates with decades of elected experience, which Josh didn't have, by emphasizing a wide and nontraditional portfolio of accomplishments across many sectors and topics. In the end, he stood out as a problem-solver in a field of politicians.

Let's quickly get up to speed on Becker's background; not the full version, that'd take too long, but some key points. He's been all over the private sector: MBA, cofounder of a venture capital firm for early-stage investments in clean tech, and founder of a legal tech accelerator. His social purpose DNA was already showing up. Same goes for the nonprofit sector: Becker cofounded Full Circle Fund, a philanthropic network that funds nonprofits and builds civic leaders. He cofounded the Stanford Board Fellows program, which trains thousands of students to serve on nonprofit boards.

Last but not least, the public sector: he worked on workforce development for the state, was a trustee at University of California at Merced, and a county commissioner on the Child Care Partnership Council in San Mateo County. The guy checks just about every box for every sector.

He is running for the state senate, most certainly to work on key challenges like climate change and education. Becker's Cross-Sector Fluency means he could really work on these challenges from a "home base" in just about any sector—public, private, or nonprofit. He reminds me of the organization-less leader mindset from Richard Woo and Alanis Valavanis. He is also the person in the room that knows how to speak everyone's language and knows which vital traits are in abundance and which are missing. He's a "glue guy." Let's focus on one challenge, climate change, and what all his experiences bring to the table:

- ▶ Private sector. He founded one of the first venture funds to focus on clean tech, so he saw a wide range of approaches, including successes and failures, and was on the board of the Clean Tech Open, a shark tank with compassion for clean energy.

- ▶ Public sector. He cofounded Cleantech and Green Business Leaders for Obama as well as the Clean Economy Network to get clean energy business leaders to engage in public policy and support candidates who are supportive of a clean energy agenda. Part of this was understanding where and why clean energy was getting traction across the county, including my home state, Iowa, where 36 percent of its power is now from wind.

- ▶ Nonprofit sector. He cofounded Full Circle Fund, which, in part, invests in nonprofits working on environmental sustainability, some that were effective and some that were not. One early grantee, Grid Alternatives, is now the nation's largest nonprofit solar installer. Another grantee was Green Cities California, which was a way for cities in the Golden State to share best practices.

In baseball, there is the expression five-tool player. It's used to describe a very unique player who excels at all five major physical aspects of the game—speed, throwing, fielding, hitting, power. Becker is a five-tool Rebuilder who is ready to work, at the highest level, on our social, economic, and health challenges in the 2020s.

Not Always the Best Timing

Michael Nutter got his Series 7 license to be an investment banker in September 1987. It was just a few weeks before Black Monday, October 19, 1987, when the stock market dropped 22.68 percent in one day. That is still the single biggest drop in market history, and by quite a ways. Second place is March 16, 2020, when it dropped nearly 13 percent.

Michael Nutter

Nutter was elected mayor of Philadelphia and took office in January 2008, just as the Great Recession of 2008–9 was emerging. You might want to keep an eye on Nutter's next major career move to see if there is an opportunity to short-sell. But don't ever short-sell Michael Nutter.

Nutter's life and career have spanned the private sector world of investment banking; the public sector in many roles across his native Philly, including as mayor; and he's been a part of numerous non-profit engagements, including Cities United and What Works Cities, that address challenges including education, public safety, and sustainability. You get the point. He is cross-sector, vertically, horizontally, and diagonally. His Cross-Sector Fluency was probably never stress-tested any more than shortly after he took office in 2008.

After he won the election, he quickly faced a $450 million, five-year budget deficit. A month later, in October, it was about $700 million, give or take tens of millions. And by the time the Phillies had won the World Series that fall and President Obama was elected, it was estimated at $1.4 billion. As a lot of us know from watching cities and states in the spring of 2020, they don't get to run deficits and print money like the federal government. Mayors and governors have to make ends meet; they have to balance their budgets. "Public-private partnerships are a key part of what saved us," Nutter told me. When used in that context of partnership, "public" means government and nonprofit sectors. It's more accurately a public-nonprofit-private partnership, but that's just too wordy.

His cross-sector dexterity ranged from "small" things like working with the Philadelphia Flyers to keep five outdoor skating rinks open and turn them over to the NHL team to operate. And big things like cutting costs and closing some public schools, while doing nothing to weaken the educational experience of their students. (See Bi Vuong, "Data Conviction," for more on this kind of work.) During the same time, by the way, they reduced homicides by 30 percent.

By the time his term was up, Philadelphia was running budget surpluses, and as a result, Philadelphia's credit rating was upgraded to the A category by the three major credit-rating agencies for the first time since the 1970s. Reversing a nearly half-a-billion-dollar deficit takes every ounce of Cross-Sector Fluency a leader can muster. To not only survive but to come out of it and give your city the opportunity to thrive. The way Nutter summed it up was "this sh– was hard."

We are walking into a decade that will be rife with monstrous deficits. Schools that were beginning to make progress will now be set back severely. We'll have the inescapable need for all three sectors to work together as they never have before. We are going to need Rebuilders who have been there, done that, and who have the tough skin and street credibility to navigate an almost impossibly complex path forward.

Every once in a while, during conversations with these leaders, they bring up a new part of their story. Sometimes it fits the main narrative and sometimes it's okay to just let the story stand on its own, one more leadership or life lesson we can all learn from. Nutter's life before he was the mayor of a major American city is a story of persevering and knowing that who each of us was "back when" doesn't determine who we will become.

Before he was mayor, he ran for city council and lost. During that campaign, his car died and he needed a loaner from a friend. At the end of that failed campaign, Nutter returned the car, *without* a radio that had been stolen and *with* $1,000 in parking tickets. At that point, nothing said here was a future mayor, not to anyone else or maybe even to himself.

The final thought I'll leave with you is this: as I've said before, many of these Rebuilders start to show up with traits earlier in life. But in Nutter's case, his journey into this kind of role took longer. He said to me, with a deep Philly chuckle, "There was nothing, I mean nothing, about me that said this guy is gonna be the mayor someday." So there is no predestination. We all have agency over the path we take and the leader we become. We have our own paths, and each one is unique. Just know that whatever your path, our nation needs you. We need leaders with the five vital traits to begin to remake and reinvent our siloed, unequal America. We need Rebuilders who are ready to take charge of change.

▶ ▶ ▶

Five Things about Cross-Sector Fluency in Our Leaders for the Future

1. They have the savvy and experience to recognize that real value exchange is now across all three sectors in both directions, back and forth between the public, private, and nonprofit sectors.
2. Cross-sector leaders are able to be flexible when needed but always have a solid foundation they work from.
3. They may have to be a translator of many layers in the process—language, culture, power, and so on.
4. In the decade ahead, this may not be the most unique, but it may be the most indispensable, of the five vital traits.
5. The best cross-sector leaders proactively search outside their most native or original sector to find new strategies and tools and experiences.

Musicals are plays, but the last collaborator is your audience, so you've got to wait 'til the last collaborator comes in before you can complete the whole collaboration.   —STEPHEN SONDHEIM

PART FOUR

Case Studies: Past, Present, and Prospective

Rebuilding America's bridges will sometimes involve repairing the deck or the superstructure, redoing part of the substructure, or replacing the piles or bridge bearings. Rebuilding America's economic, health, and social foundations will take everything we've got, because we're rebuilding not just the parts but the whole bridge.

Rebuilding is not sexy. For most people, it's way more exciting to build something new. Plenty of people want to put up a building on a campus with their name on it, but far fewer want to endow a building's maintenance or remodeling costs. People love to do ribbon-cutting ceremonies, but they don't congregate around a building to celebrate its repairs.

It will take leaders—individuals, teams, companies, communities—with all five of these traits brought fully to bear on the problems at hand. All five work together, in part because they balance one another and because you need all of these traits and fluencies at the table of positive change. You can't take one of them away any more than you can take away one part of a bridge you are trying to fix.

As a way of trying to show what the impact can be when these five vital traits and Rebuilders like these thirty-eight are brought together, let's look at three case studies: (1) a retrospective case when things didn't work out as planned, (2) a current-day case study that was successful, and (3) a prospective, hypothetical case study for what is possible. The intent isn't to tell three stories that are perfect but to illustrate and bring to life how the five vital traits of Rebuilders have, do, and could play a seminal role in community and corporate change.

Retrospective Case Study One: Fell Short

Let's look at homelessness in Seattle. As I said at the very start, homelessness is a challenge that directly affects the nonprofit, public, and private sectors. It impacts quality of life, public safety, and economic development. I've lived it as a person who worked in downtown Seattle for seventeen years, twelve in the Belltown area and the last five in Pioneer Square. It is a community and corporate problem that has gotten undeniably worse, by any measure. No matter your lens or beliefs, homelessness in Seattle in the last ten years has become a scar on the city's pride, humanity, economy, and future.

Let's talk through how the five vital traits came into play. In 2005, a lot of well-intended, smart, committed people at the United Way of King County publicly aspired, and had the good courage, to lead the "Ten-Year Campaign to End Homelessness." As you read this, keep in mind that estimates are for homelessness to grow as much as 40 percent in 2021, due to the economic and health effects of COVID.[1] Forty percent in twelve months. Here was Ordinance 15284 that was signed by a number of excellent people on September 19, 2005:

KING COUNTY

Signature Report

September 19, 2005

1200 King County Courthouse
516 Third Avenue
Seattle, WA 98104

Ordinance 15284

Proposed No. 2005-0371.1   **Sponsors** Patterson, Lambert, Edmonds and
Phillips

1	AN ORDINANCE adopting a ten-year plan to end
2	homelessness in King County, designating the Committee
3	to End Homelessness as the local homeless and housing
4	task force pursuant to state law and the body to coordinate
5	and oversee implementation of the ten-year plan, accepting
6	an initial county action plan in support of the ten-year plan
7	and committing county health, human services and law and
8	justice programs to work with each other and the
9	Committee to End Homelessness to achieve the ten-year
10	plan goals.

Ten years later, on May 2, 2015, they posted a letter that, to their credit, candidly stated, "Despite our community's commitment to the vision of a future without homelessness the problem has gotten worse. We've struggled with forces over which we have no control. We've also struggled to change our approaches and realign funding to support our vision."

I'm offering a secondhand perspective here on how I think the vital traits of Rebuilders could have made for a different outcome for the county and region I call home.

Let's start with the most obvious. We know it takes leaders with Data Conviction. In the case of the ten-year campaign, the data they focused on was moment-in-time counts one night each year. That was standard practice at the time but wasn't nearly enough. The problem got more complicated in the ensuing years, especially in a housing market like Seattle. Regardless of the surrounding economics, they didn't have the right kind of data.

There is no doubt they started out trying to get everyone involved in the solution, across sectors. But no one can look at what played out and say we got it right for King County. The nonprofit sector continues to be too splintered on service delivery to this day. There were some public-private partnerships going on, but there just wasn't a collective enough, holistic buy-in across all three sectors. There still isn't to this day. We are still lacking critical mass in Cross-Sector Fluency.

When it comes to Complexity Capacity, I'll admit this is partly conjecture, a supposition. The leadership at the United Way on the project was Jon F. and Vince M. The cochairs of the initial committee were Humberto A. and Dan B. The two primary signatories were Larry P. and Ron S. I know more than half of those men personally. Every one of them has been effective and successful in their lives. And they have one common trait—they're men.

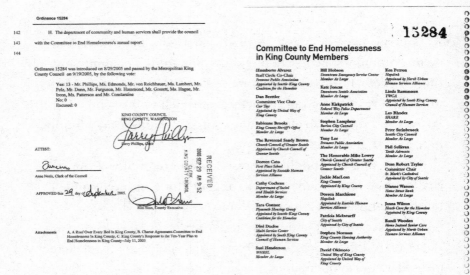

There were certainly women in the room, on staff and committees, but the initial visible, primary leadership was all male. It's not a stretch to believe there were not enough nonlinear, complexity-strong women in the room when the *initial* strategies were being set. There is no way for me to ever prove cause and effect, and I'm sure there are plenty of stories that would plausibly contradict my opinion here. But the correlation is 100 percent.

When it comes to 24-7 Authenticity, I don't doubt this for a moment. Again, I know these leaders and they were committed. They deserve every plaudit for having the courage to take on the problem in a way no one else had before.

And when it comes to enough Generosity Mindset, I don't have enough to say.

Having a shortage of at least three of the five traits on the team and in the plan in 2005 is a plausible explanation for at least part of the campaign's downfall. There is no doubt that the steep increase in housing prices over that same decade was a major factor as well.

To say watching homelessness play out the way it has in Seattle is heartbreaking is a gross understatement. Almost from the day our team at Social Venture Partners Seattle moved so excitedly to our new digs in Pioneer Square in 2010, the problem started deteriorating. From something "relatively small" at that time to something that started to almost take over. I remember the first time I went into our office one morning; I was one of the first in the building, a shared office space at 220 Second Avenue South, and found feces in the doorway. That was around 2012.

Not long thereafter was the first morning I walked in and there was a homeless person lying in the doorway. Not long thereafter was the first time there was a tent encampment in the doorway blocking my way in.

My purpose in this story is not to throw anyone under the bus; it's just to use a real situation as a case study. *To anyone in King County that I offended, thank you for your awesome efforts and my apologies for any inaccuracies and slights.* As we move forward into the 2020s, we need to have new leaders around the table.

Where we are today is not a long way ahead of where we were in 2005. There are a lot of good people around the table. The city and county made an announcement in 2019 about working together, and as of summer 2020, too many people I know say we are stuck in the same Seattle process that bogs us down so often. I can see many pieces are in place or in better shape, but not enough and not soon enough.

Retrospective Case Study Two: Reached Its Goal

Let's look briefly at one of Built for Zero's recent successes—ending veteran homelessness in Chattanooga, Tennessee, in October 2019. You can read their case study,[2] but let's understand, between the words of some of the key leaders, where our five leadership traits showed up:

- ▶ 24-7 Authenticity. Someone needed to step forward and acknowledge their premature end to homelessness in 2016 was not truly the case; it wasn't functional zero yet. Chalk that up to the original Team Leads, Mark Williams and Emma Beers.

- ▶ Complexity Capacity. "We were able to say: Where do we focus our efforts? What was an issue that was happening because there was a real barrier that someone was facing? What were we not thinking creatively enough about?" said Beers, Director of System Performance.

▶ Generosity Mindset. "The team became so collaborative, through a regular practice of meeting called 'case conferencing,' where they were aggressively setting goals and taking an all-hands-on-deck approach to meeting them," said Eddie Turner, the Built for Zero coach for Chattanooga. "Agencies were helping each other out and taking steps to house each other's clients," said two people on the core team in Chattanoogan, Wendy Winters and Casey Tinker.

▶ Data Conviction. More than three years before they reached true "functional zero," Community Solutions' definition for zero homelessness, the city met a federal government definition of zero in 2016. But that one wasn't sufficient, much like Seattle's wasn't several years prior. It took everyone's commitment to and conviction about data, and to look at it in a new way—real-time, person-specific—to reach their ultimate goal.

▶ Cross-Sector Fluency. They had all three sectors at the table; we know you can't make change happen now without a full table.

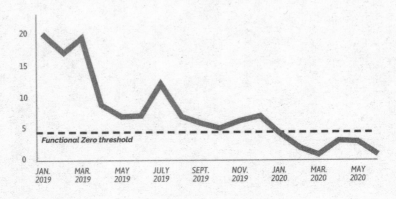

Actively Homeless Veterans

Prospective Case Study Three— The Potential for Our Future

Let's use our imagination. It doesn't take a lot after you've read about these thirty-eight leaders. Suppose there is a social challenge in a city or region that has been intractable for years, for decades. One that is going to be greatly exacerbated by the events of 2020. Let's take poverty and economic development, particularly in inner-city communities, which have been the hardest hit. We know we need leaders that

▸ will state the problem, own it, stand up to those that would minimize it or ignore the undercurrents of racial inequity— leaders like Michael McAfee or Debbie Little with 24-7 Authenticity who are willing to step forward, name the full problem, and commit to seeing real change and no less.

▸ have lived in and dealt with that kind of complexity—people like Jennifer Blatz and Erica Valliant with Complexity Capacity, who have dealt with multiple cities across multiple states, have a lived experience at every level of the problem, and have the collective experience, wisdom, and eyes-on-the-prize mindset to co-create real solutions.

▶ have the ability to hold the table, bring everyone to it, and make sure everyone feels shared ownership—leaders with a Generosity Mindset like Cecilia Guiterrez or Apryle Brodie, who have been doing just that in communities across America, including Miami and Los Angeles.

▶ will stare down the real data, the right data that tells the only story that will lead to a solution—leaders with Data Conviction like Jennifer Park or Jeff Edmondson who have spent years of their careers working with cities and communities to know how to do just that.

▶ have Cross-Sector Fluency and can fully engage the non-profit, public, and private sectors and bring all of the players together—Rebuilders like David Risher or Cheryl Dorsey who have done it time and time again in their careers.

The place where Rebuilders like these leaders come together most effectively might be a major urban city, but it's as or more likely to be a midsized American community like Memphis, Tennessee, or Dayton, Ohio, or even a rural region like Dreama Gentry's Berea County, Kentucky. We will see what the future holds.

It's sort of a "dream team." Remember, it isn't just the right individuals, it's the right whole team. We need all of those vital traits at the same community table together. We will not make real progress without Rebuilders who bring all five vital traits to bear on a complex problem that needs a cross-sector solution.

Just to put an exclamation on that last point: having *most*, but not *all*, of the right leaders is sort of like saying we have a semitrailer that has seventeen awesome wheels but the eighteenth is from my kid's bicycle. The economic, social, and health challenges in the decade ahead for America absolutely require eighteen-wheelers. If we show up with "almost enough" to go after our challenges, we will fall short. We can't have flat or missing tires in the 2020s. Maybe that was okay in the second half of the twentieth century, but not today. And definitely not for the challenges facing us in the decade ahead.

PART FIVE

Our Possible Futures

Your community needs you. When I say your community, I mean
your rec league, the church, your youth group, and most of all your
school. They need you. Most importantly, building your community
is how you change the world. Be the first generation to embrace
your responsibility: to *rebuild* your community. Class of 2020, the
world has changed. You will determine how we will *rebuild*.

—LEBRON JAMES,
speaking to graduating seniors, May 2020

I went downtown to Seattle on May 30, 2020, to march in support
of George Floyd, deeply saddened and angry about what happened. I was hopeful at the chance to stand alongside fellow
citizens who felt the way I did and wanted to see real damn change
this time. Within five minutes of standing at Sixth and Olive, a few
flash bangs from the police went off. If you've seen them only on TV
or online, you don't understand the initial feeling of fear and shock.

A few minutes later, I was keeping an eye on my two sons standing
over by a light post. A guy next to them grabbed the steel street trash
can and pushed it over. It banged on the ground and rolled into the

middle of the intersection. Then he walked across the street like nothing had happened. There he met two "friends," one of whom had a small wagon full of something that I couldn't see clearly from fifty feet away.

One of the three put on a gas mask. The other two grabbed various items and then the three of them dispersed. A few minutes later, I saw the trash-can guy walk along Sixth Street, in front of Nordstrom's, where three police cars were parked. He graffitied all three of them in broad daylight. It seemed like there was something he was throwing at or in or around the three cars. A few minutes later, all three were on fire. And a few more minutes later, one of the other three men I had observed fifteen minutes earlier was smashing out windows in the restaurant across the street. (Yes, I sent all the photos to the Seattle Police Dept. and none of those three white men were there to do anything positive for Black Lives Matter.)

I came to town hopeful and seeking optimism and determination for change. I left confused and angry. I think a lot of us came into the twenty-first century hopeful and optimistic, and we've arrived in 2021 confused and angry. The question for each of us, the leaders and readers of this book and the Rebuilders across America, is what are we going to do with that confusion and anger now?

Everything happening—a global pandemic, a senseless murder and worldwide protest, an election of epic importance, and who knows what else—is ratcheting up the risk and growing the urgency of the opportunity. This is the next huge step in our nation's 244-year experiment.

Should we be hopeful or daunted? Should we look at the increasingly steep challenges ahead and be despondent or determined? As we look at the scale and complexity of the task of rebuilding, should we be disheartened or believe in our ability to muster the resources to rebuild as America has many times before?

In the Introduction, I made the statement that I am worried about America in the dark of night but fundamentally optimistic in

the light of day. These thirty-eight leaders are the number-one reason to feel hopeful, not despondent; to feel things are possible, not
improbable; and to believe that there is a way forward, not just a
sense that our best days are behind us or that we want to return to
some glory days that either never existed or are now long gone. The
Rebuilders you have read about in this book are up to that challenge. So are millions of Americans . . . and you.

 IN RECENT YEARS, states have preferred
design-build contracts to carry out the rebuilding of bridges. Design and construction teams working
together from the start. Complications and contradictions are
resolved internally and quickly so that the project can proceed
with minimum delay.

With government funding for infrastructure projects being
so tight, a financing alternative has arisen in the form of
public-private partnerships. Private investors assume the responsibility for financing and building a bridge, and the investors are granted the right to collect tolls, believing they will
realize a good return on investment.

New contract arrangements and creative financing are being used to repair and replace aging bridges more economically, quickly, and safely.[1] Some of the same kind of creative
approaches and strategies for reusing existing resources to
rebuild America's bridges can be a very useful example to
guide and inform how we rebuild our communities. And no
doubt we will need the five traits of Rebuilders in making the
best possible use of our nonprofit, public, and private sectors' constrained resources in order to build a bridge to a
better future.

The metaphor of bridges has been our guide. What kind of future are we rebuilding a bridge to? There are clearly dystopian versions we see previewed before our eyes every single day. There are other possible futures that are powerful and positive and transformational.

Let's talk about what those futures could be in these next three chapters through three different lenses:

1. How this can all play out globally, not just domestically
2. How this thinking on leadership applies to all three sectors: public, private, and nonprofit
3. Whether our individual and collective mindset should be pessimistic or optimistic

There are decades when nothing happens; and there are weeks when decades happen.   —VLADIMIR LENIN

CHAPTER TEN

In a Post-COVID-19 World

Historically, pandemics have forced humans to break with the past and imagine their world anew. This one is no different. It is a portal, a gateway between one world and the next. We can choose to walk through it, dragging the carcasses of our prejudice and hatred, our avarice, our data banks and dead ideas, our dead rivers and smoky skies behind us. Or we can walk through lightly, with little luggage, ready to imagine another world. And ready to fight for it.

—ARUNDHATI ROY,
Indian author, *Financial Times*

"Ready to imagine another world. And ready to fight for it." That is the right mindset for leaders for the future. These times have given, if anything, even more fuel to the fire. Our nation truly feels like it hangs in the balance in the 2020s. And the implications expand far beyond our borders.

So many times, over the course of my life, I've traveled overseas, for business or pleasure, and heard the same message, unprompted, again and again. Once from a cabbie in New Zealand, from friends in Canada, from a hotel clerk in Italy, in a group discussion in Japan. The comments were along the lines of "We care more about your presidential election than we do our own. We don't always like what America does, but we need America. We want America to be strong and to lead."

America is imperfect, has made way more mistakes than we should, and has abused our power far too often. But we are, especially now, the right "superpower" to be leading a post-COVID world. As damaged as some of our ideals are, we still stand for freedom and democracy as powerfully as any nation around the globe.

In the 1990s, America was leading and the world was moving ahead in powerful, historic ways. The Berlin Wall came down, democracies were ascendant, and a global technology revolution seemed to make almost all things possible. Since then, we've gone from Gorbachev to Putin, from Lula to Bolsonaro, from Xiaoping to Jinping.

The work we've been talking about Rebuilders doing isn't geopolitics, but it's hard to overstate how much the decade ahead matters, not just for America, but for the entire global community we are a part of.

Pandemics can catalyze social change. People, businesses, and institutions have been remarkably quick to adopt or call for practices that they might once have dragged their heels on. . . . Perhaps the nation will learn that preparedness isn't just about masks, vaccines, and tests but also about fair labor policies and stable and equal health care.   —ED YONG, the *Atlantic*

CHAPTER ELEVEN

It's about All Three Sectors

"For generations, and most successfully in the Depression's aftermath, the United States has used public-private partnerships to drive the country's economic expansion, allowing entrepreneurs and companies to take advantage of the long-term planning and financial strength of Uncle Sam. This is the solution that must no longer be overlooked. What we need right now are public-private partnerships on a scale not attempted since the Depression." One could guess a lot of people who could have written that in 2020, but likely not Barry Ritholtz. He's probably most widely known for *Bailout Nation,* in which he decried bailouts for, among others, Chrysler in 1980, Long-Term Capital Management in 1998, and the failing banks of 2008–9. Apparently, Ritholtz thinks we are living through different times than we ever would have thought possible.

Public–private (and nonprofit) partnerships are a concept kind of like corporate social responsibility. They started out as sort of a PR thing in the '80s and '90s, then started to take some substantive, if ineffective steps in the first decade of the 2000s. And today, cross-sector partnerships will be part of the solutions to many challenges. Let's look at how Rebuilders are relevant to all three sectors. I'll lay out three or four suggestions for each, starting with the private sector.

Private Sector

▶ Hire them. We talked about it time and again throughout Part II and in many of the stories of the leaders in the Profits versus Purpose section in chapter 9, that is, the increasing degree of integration of companies with their communities. We were heading in that direction, and with COVID and the racial equity movement that started off this decade so profoundly, we are now at a point of no return.

▶ Companies need Rebuilders with Cross-Sector Fluency at all levels in all departments. We don't want to bolt cross-sector leaders onto companies transactionally or organize them in one organizational silo or department. We want them in all the normal functions, in all departments, all across the company. We need cross-sector product managers and salespeople and distribution managers; it goes on and on. It's good to have a team or leader responsible for the integration across a community, but even more valuable long term is integrating this mindset into all of your people. Not only so you'll have better "community relations,"

but because you will be a more effective company,
period.

▶ Do the right thing . . . for the bottom line. Whether
you are part of a company that signed on to the
Business Roundtable commitment or not, go live those
principles. Not just for the right, moral reasons but
because the marketplace and consumers, both
business-to-consumer or business-to-business, will punish
you if you do not. Twenty to thirty years ago, it started to
become a popular notion that consumers would take the
environment or corporate social responsibility into
consideration when making purchasing decisions. At first,
it wasn't in a big way. In the last five to ten years, it's
become a real part of more and more consumer
purchase decisions.

▶ Going forward, it might still be a plus, but we've crossed
over. If you are not living those principles, it will be a
negative. Behaving in a way that is driven by stakeholders,
not just shareholders, is the ante now, not an advantage,
and if you don't ante up, you will not be in the game
long term.

▶ Take your professional development to the next level. Use
these traits in your hiring, team building, and professional
development strategies. Don't just let this be a theoretical
exercise. These are identifiable qualities and skill sets that
you can target with new hires and build in to ongoing
professional development.

Cross-Sector Fluency is the number one of all five traits that *private* sector companies will need to build in the decade ahead.

Public Sector

▶ Play the integrator role. The public sector can see themselves as more than "just" the government that works in partnership with the other two sectors. They have the unique opportunity, in place in communities, to play more of an integrator and convener role. Not the lead role but the integrator role, the one that brings the private and nonprofit and public sectors together. When it comes to playing this role, nonprofits often don't have enough scale, and the private sector doesn't have the expertise. The public sector is pretty uniquely situated to play this role if they will be intentional and humble in the way they go about it. That is, use some 24-7 Authenticity, a Generosity Mindset . . .

▶ Think data, data, data. Keep going all-in on data like Phoenix and other American cities that have attained a What Works Cities certification.[1] From what I've seen, city and county governments can start to turn the perception of its citizens in powerful ways, but it will take time. If they do it right, they can start to work their way back up from that 11 percent confidence rate we talked about in chapter 2, "Where We Are."

▶ Make your own story. See "One Last Rebuilder Story" at the end. Consider entities like Challenge Seattle and roles like the one Chris Gregoire played for COVID in the greater Seattle area. People like Felipe Moreno, Apryle Brodie, Nicollette Staton, and Michael Nutter have started to show that kind of leadership. Build on those lessons learned.

24-7 Authenticity is the number one of all five traits that *public* sector entities will need to build most in the decade ahead.

Nonprofit Sector

▶ Embrace the data. I'm not saying it's ever easy; it's not. Entities like Built for Zero and StriveTogether have proven nonprofits can use data powerfully. And it does make a profound difference. We have to invest in the nonprofit sector's ability to use data at scale. Follow the list of best practices we laid out in the "Is There an Approach to Data That Matters?" section in chapter 8. There are road maps. This isn't a path with no navigation to follow.

▶ Think bigger. We can't afford to think small or come from scarcity anymore. Don't confuse this with being big and corporate and not driven by and for your local community. As politically incorrect as it sometimes sounds, the nonprofit sector is too splintered. There are too many nonprofits, which is preventing us from scaling to meet the challenges we are facing. To be clear, private sector and public sector funders of nonprofits are just as splintered and have just as much, probably more, work to do to be ready to be less splintered.

▶ Use your voice. Along the same lines as each of the other two sectors, leverage what you know. Recognize the on-the-ground, community-connected knowledge and credibility you uniquely have that the public, and private, sectors just can't deliver as consistently. Focus on the people, not the systems created to deliver to them. Systems should organize around the individuals, not the other way around, which is how it's mostly been.

Data Conviction is the number one of all five traits that *nonprofit* sector organizations will need to build most in the decade ahead.

P.S. to the foundation/funder/philanthropy side of the community change equation. In reaction to COVID, a lot of foundations signed on to some exceptional and unique practices that fit the urgent times. For example, a pledge led by the Ford Foundation[2] (whose regular practices, prior to COVID, have been moving in this direction and providing crucial leadership) is a call to action to philanthropies everywhere. The call is to address the unanticipated effects of this global crisis as its social and economic implications unfold, so grantees can move quickly to serve the communities most affected. Some of the practices called out and adopted include:

► Loosen or eliminate the restrictions on current grants.
► Make any new grants as unrestricted as possible, so that nonprofit partners have maximum flexibility to respond to a crisis.
► Communicate proactively and regularly about our decision-making and response to provide helpful information while not asking more of grantee partners.
► Commit to listening to our partners, especially to those communities least heard, lifting up their voices and experiences to inform public discourse and our own decision-making.
► Support, as appropriate, grantee partners advocating for important public policy changes.
► Learn from these emergency practices and share what they teach us about effective partnership and philanthropic support, so we may consider adjusting our practices more fundamentally in the future, in more stable times, based on all we learn.

Let me say this bluntly and plainly: for God's sake, those are all *the right practices for all times*. Do not go back. Stay with these "emergency" practices.

The dual imperative of our time is to save lives and safeguard live-lihoods—and governments around the world are pulling out all the stops to do so. The resulting ramp-up of relief and stimulus spending to unprecedented levels has occurred just as tax revenues have slumped. As a result, government deficits worldwide could reach $9 trillion to $11 trillion in 2020, and a cumulative total of as much as $30 trillion by 2023.

Governments will need to find ways to manage these unprecedented deficits without crippling their economies. It is this challenge which creates the need for the great balancing act: managing the $30 trillion deficit while restoring economic growth. We believe that this can be done—but it will require governments and the private sector to work together like never before to lay the foundations for a new social contract and to begin shaping a postcrisis era of shared, sustainable prosperity.   —MCKINSEY & CO., June 16, 2020[3]

CHAPTER TWELVE

Optimism versus Pessimism

So, in this convulsive moment, let's not say, "This isn't who we are."
The right question is, "Who do we want to be?"

—JON MEACHAM

n the fall of 2019, Rachel Maddow came to Seattle on her book tour. My wife and I attended, sitting in a row about halfway back in a packed Benaroya Hall. She was compelling and articulate. It was a home-court crowd if there ever was one. Clapping, cheering, calling out, it was a semi-revival atmosphere. Until the next-to-last question.

The interviewer asked her what we need to do after the election the following November, regardless of who wins the presidency. Maddow's response was something to the effect that "we all have to reach back across the aisle and across the fence to find ways to work and live together again." At that moment, the crowd turned to skeptical murmurs, a few mild catcalls, and polite listening, but the revival was over for a minute or two.

Maddow was right. No matter how big the economic, social, health, and political divides feel to most of us, we have to build bridges back across all of those divides.

If Michael McAfee can sit at the same table of wealth and power that once pushed him away, then we can rebuild a bridge to a better economy that brings lower income households into the middle class.

If Andy Lipkis can bring together the water and sanitation and flood control departments, whose missions literally flow in opposite directions, then we can rebuild bridges to make health more attainable by everyone, not just for some.

If Kathy Calvin can bring nations globally together around seventeen sustainable development goals, then we can rebuild bridges to make more social progress on women's rights and racial equity in America.

There is a lot being written these days about different possible scenarios for the American future, for the decade ahead. Let me offer these three:

1. *It is the beginning of the end.* The unequal and siloed America of the first twenty years of this century just keeps going. Like every empire that came before it—Roman, Ottoman, British, and so on—the 2020s are the decade when American influence and standing in the world truly comes to an end and global leadership is largely ceded to more authoritarian governments.

2. *We muddle along.* The increase in inequities and division find an equilibrium; it becomes the status quo for the 2020s. We slow or stop the decline, but we never make real progress on our economic, health, and social megachallenges.

3. *We meet the moment.* The intensity of COVID and our eventual coming out of it showed us our common humanity. The horror, aftermath, and national movement

around racial equity and social justice wasn't just a
fleeting moment. Both of those seminal moments really
did change America for the better.

It's not a surprise that the number-one key to America meeting
the moment is leadership, the kind that these Rebuilders bring to
their work and lives. There are bridges—decks, substructures,
bearings, superstructures, piers—to be rebuilt. There is a nation to
be rebuilt in the decade ahead. It's not just that it's an opportunity
or a high-minded aspiration. We have no choice. We have to get
this right. We have to have leaders ready to take charge of the
change all around us.

We need the economic progress of the second half of the twentieth century without the racial and gender inequities that exist to
this day. We need to see real progress in the health of America
without the rural-urban inequities that widened in the past twenty
years. And we need to see more social progress for women and
people of color, period.

> At this crazy, frightening, chaotic moment, it is possible to reach
> across old lines and create new alliances, to reemphasize that most
> Americans really do share the same values of economic fairness
> and equality before the law, and to rebuild a government of the
> people, by the people, and for the people. The old world is cer-
> tainly dying, but the shape of the new world struggling to be born
> is not yet determined.   —HEATHER COX RICHARDSON,
>   professor of history at Boston College

One Last Rebuilder Story

This is the story of a leader, of a lot of leaders, who brought together
the best of who they were in a time that required absolutely nothing

less. There was a lot that could have gone very differently without the right people in the room in greater Seattle. And there was a master of complexity in the middle of it all.

As of Saturday morning, February 29, there were fifty-seven active known cases of COVID across the United States. Now known as the good ol' days. It was the night before the first American would die from the coronavirus, about fifty miles north of downtown Seattle. The news that weekend around here was covering a handful of cases, person by person: "A woman in her 40s who is employed at the facility . . . is being treated at Overlake Hospital. The second case is a woman in her 70s who is a LifeCare resident. She is being treated at Evergreen Health Hospital in Kirkland and is in serious condition. In the past 24 hours, health officials have confirmed five total cases in the state, including the man who died."[1]

But things hadn't begun to ramp up yet, still at the frog-in-a-frying-pan stage.

Chris Gregoire is the former attorney general and governor of Washington State. Today she is the CEO of Challenge Seattle, which

Chris Gregoire

"harnesses the leadership, resources, and talent of its private sector member companies to find solutions and inspire collective action for the greater good."

On Tuesday, February 25, Gregoire had requested data from scientists at the Fred Hutchinson Cancer Research Center in Seattle.[2] She wasn't 100 percent sure what she was looking at yet or whether to believe the data. It was telling a radically, urgently different story than the rest of the world was yet absorbing. We were still two weeks away from the NBA shutting down, which honestly seemed to be one of the instigating events when America finally "got it."

That night Gregoire called up her board chair, Susan Mullaney, and explained what she was looking at and her reticence about sharing the data too fast. Mullaney was just as stunned. No one had seen health data like this before, and it wasn't out of a sci-fi book. What do you do with information that is just not on anyone's radar yet but you are pretty sure it's right? Gregoire said she was "kind of scared to share it." Governor Gregoire rarely fears anything, believe me. That is what is called a moment of truth.

The regular meeting of her Challenge Seattle board was later that day. That board[3] comprises the CEOs who lead the companies that make the greater Seattle area economy move—Microsoft, Starbucks, Alaska Airlines, Costco, Kaiser Washington, and so on. There was 100 percent attendance. Gregoire and Mullaney were holding back the data at first, but as the conversation moved on, the two of them knew they needed to put the science and data on the table. They all saw the same data and agreed to follow the science.

Five days later, on March 1, they called a non-optional Sunday conference call for all board members, and it was again 100 percent attendance. The next day, Satya Nadella, CEO at Microsoft, told tens of thousands of Microsoft employees in the Seattle area that they *could* work at home. The next day, they *insisted* that workers work from home. That was March 3, 2020.

A few days later, lots of other cities and states around the nation started to get the same information, but few of them moved yet like Seattle and Washington State. New York and New Jersey as well, as they executed precautions when they shifted into high gear, lost a week or two at the start, which proved so costly.

Gregoire was on the board at the Fred Hutchinson Cancer Research Center and, back on February 25, she was looking at data from a barely known researcher, Trevor Bedford, who looks exactly like you'd expect a brilliant nerd to look. Before the pandemic, Bedford was best known in a small circle of bioinformatics specialists who use rapid genomic analysis to monitor pathogens (if you know what that means, you're probably reading the wrong book). Today, he has a Twitter following of more than 250,000.

He was one of the first researchers to see what was coming. His models showed numbers that would have seemed crazy on January 15 and three months later tracked a gruesome state of the pandemic.

Chris Gregoire will tell you in a heartbeat that it was a total team effort, and it definitely had to be. I also know she worked fifteen-hour days, seven days a week after February 25. That's about fourteen hundred hours, give or take a hundred cups of coffee, over the next three months. It's hard to fathom the number of inputs and data and vectors coming at her. Complexity on steroids. Just consider that there was

- ▶ no road map. There is knowledge about Ebola, SARS, and other viruses around Seattle, but this was a different playbook.
- ▶ unceasing nonlinear information coming at her from scientists, businesspeople, mayors, and governors.
- ▶ the need to adapt hourly at the start and maybe daily by summer.
- ▶ a massive volume of information to be sorted and shared.

She was the right leader for the moment. What was the impact of Chris Gregoire's Complexity Capacity? It's hard to even fathom. In simple terms, Washington State was number one on the national list for total cases for the first few weeks of March; now it's number twenty-seven (as of late October 2020). This math can get a little squeamish, but we are looking at saved human lives as the metric of impact.

Let's don't compare greater Seattle to metropolitan New York or northern New Jersey. They are denser, more compressed populations. If we look at the urban areas of Massachusetts, Rhode Island,

Connecticut, and Michigan—of similar size and scope to Puget Sound—they had deaths per capita at a rate four to six times greater than Seattle. So far, we in Seattle have lost about 2,300 lives (as of late October), so doing the simple math says that Gregoire and the work she did and her Complexity Capacity saved about five thousand human lives.

I've had the chance to get to know Gregoire over the last five years. She is a forceful personality. One of my personal "litmus" questions for someone like her is, "I know they have one mouth; do they have two ears?" Indeed, she does. She can listen as forcefully as she can talk. You can't have a high capacity for complexity if you don't.

At the end of our recent chat, she told me, "This has been the most unprecedented public-private partnership I've seen in my career." You'd have to have exceedingly high Cross-Sector Fluency as well to make a statement like that. Along with Trish Millines and Dreama Gentry, Gregoire is probably the closest Rebuilder I can see who possesses all five vital traits. Yes, the fact that they are women is not a coincidence. I've already told you . . . you better have women in the room. And thank goodness for Washington State, Chris Gregoire was in the room.

AFTERWORD

We have all struggled, and will continue, to make meaning out of 2020. Sitting here on November 1, 2020, we may well not be halfway through the impact of 2020. Leslie Dwight penned a poem that caught on in the summer of 2020:

What if 2020 is the year we've been waiting for?
A year so uncomfortable, so painful, so scary, so raw—
that it finally forces us to grow,
A year that screams so loud, finally awakening us
from our ignorant slumber.
A year we finally accept the need for change.
Declare change. Work for change. Become the change.
A year we finally band together, instead of
pushing each other further apart.
2020 isn't canceled, but rather
the most important year of them all.

Those words are no doubt inspiring for most. Others felt that it reflects the privilege of not having to feel as much pain as others. Dwight, who is white, was thirteen years old when she learned that her father, who died when she was just a newborn, had actually died by suicide. That revelation taught her the importance of resilience during trying times, so her words are born of her own personal pain. As inspiring (or not) as one might read and feel those words, there is no way that any three words say more about the meaning of 2020 and the decade ahead of us than "I can't breathe."

Even the act of typing those words feels like it minimizes the pain and suffering and utterly tragic end of life that George Floyd faced for his last eight minutes, forty-six seconds. There is no way to feel other than deep anger and sadness. There is eventually a way to feel determined, too. For some it will never cease to cause the deepest pain, but for some of those same people, those will perhaps also be the words that finally began to change racism in America.

I didn't write this book to talk about how to solve systemic racism in America. I'm not qualified to do so. I can say this: the kind of leaders it will take to begin to make real progress on systemic, racial inequities are some of the same Rebuilders it will take to make true lasting progress on the five megachallenges we framed at the start of this book.

We are ultimately working on the common underlying condition of an acceleratingly unequal and siloed America. We can all agree to work for a better future and take charge of change in all the right ways. We can all live our lives in a way that can lead to a more equal, interconnected nation in the 2020s. We can all aspire to lead in a way that will mean George Floyd did not die in vain. We can all be Rebuilders.

I could not have known at the time but, when I was five years old, some five hundred miles northeast of my rural Texas home, a young man named John Lewis crossed a bridge for me. That historic day, like many others in his extraordinary life, Congressman Lewis endured the unconscionable to challenge and change the conscience of the nation he loved—to make our union more perfect; to bring us closer to our founding ideals; so that little black children, like me, could pursue our American dreams.

Late last night, Congressman Lewis, my hero, crossed another bridge, from elder to ancestor, with characteristic courage and grace. In marking this passage, we need not idealize Congressman Lewis beyond who he was: a founder of—a righteous force for—a more American United States and a fairer, better world.

—DARREN WALKER, CEO, Ford Foundation

NOTES

Introduction

1. "Homelessness Is Solvable," Community Solutions homepage. Accessed at https://community.solutions/.
2. "Built for Zero," Community Solutions, 2020. Accessed at https://community.solutions/our-solutions/built-for-zero/.
3. "Bridge Report," infographic, American Road and Transportation Builders Association, April 2, 2020. Accessed at https://artbabridgereport.org/.
4. The definition of civil society—a community of citizens linked by common interests and collective activity, i.e., like the United States of America.
5. Chris Woodford, "Bridges," Explain That Stuff, last updated June 23, 2019. Accessed at https://www.explainthatstuff.com/bridges.html.
6. Jim Collins, "Level 5 Leadership," Jim Collins homepage. Accessed at https://www.jimcollins.com/concepts/level-five-leadership.html.
7. "And Now, What's Next," *Seth's Blog*, April 27, 2020. Accessed at https://seths.blog/2020/04/and-now-whats-next/.

Part I

1. "LeBron James Greatest Block of All Time," YouTube video, uploaded June 19, 2016, by TWO3. Accessed at https://www.youtube.com/watch?v=F1mWjbn6a18.
2. "Changing a City's Recycling Habits with City of Phoenix Public Works' Felipe Moreno," *Impact Podcast with John Shegerian*, August 18, 2014. Accessed at https://impactpodcast.com/guest/city-of-phoenix-public-works-felipe-moreno/.
3. "City Manager's Performance Measurement Dashboard," City of Phoenix. Accessed at https://www.phoenix.gov/citymanager/dashboard.
4. "Phoenix Graduates First Class of Garbage Truck Driver Apprentices," City of Phoenix, March 2, 2018. Accessed at https://www.phoenix.gov/news/publicworks/1970.

5. Paul Shoemaker, *Can't Not Do: The Compelling Social Drive That Changes Our World* (Wiley, 2015).

6. "Volatility, Uncertainty, Complexity, and Ambiguity," Wikipedia. Accessed at https://en.wikipedia.org/wiki/Volatility,_uncertainty,_complexity _and_ambiguity.

7. "The Value of Volunteer Time Announced," Independent Sector homepage. Accessed at www.independentsector.org.

8. "Talk: Oliver Wendell Holmes Jr.," Wikiquote. Accessed at https:// en.wikiquote.org/wiki/Talk:Oliver_Wendell_Holmes_Jr.

9. Communities in Schools homepage. Accessed at https://www .communitiesinschools.org/.

10. TAF homepage. Accessed at www.techaccess.org.

Part II

1. John Mitchell, "Main Parts of a Bridge—Explained," Engineering Clicks, October 30, 2017. Accessed at https://www.engineeringclicks.com/main -parts-of-a-bridge/.

Chapter 1

1. Jordan Weissmann, "60 Years of American Economic History, Told in 1 Graph," *Atlantic*, August 23, 2012. Accessed at https://www.theatlantic .com/business/archive/2012/08/60-years-of-american-economic-history -told-in-1-graph/261503/.

2. Max Roser, Esteban Ortiz-Ospina, and Hannah Ritchie, "Life Expectancy," Our World in Data, 2013 (revised October 2019). Accessed at https:// ourworldindata.org/life-expectancy.

3. Scott Harrah, "American Medical Milestones Since Independence in 1776," University of Medicine and Health Sciences, July 3, 2013. Accessed at https://www.umhs-sk.org/blog/american-medical-milestones-since -1776/.

4. "1964 Margaret Chase Smith Presidential Campaign Announcement," January 27, 1964, as archived on Northeast Historic Film/C-SPAN. Accessed at https://www.c-span.org/video/?325362-1/1964-margaret -chase-smith-presidential-campaign-announcement.

5. Maggie Parker, "Meryl Streep: Women 'Will Not Be Bullied,'" *TIME*, April 11, 2016. Accessed at https://time.com/4288512/meryl-streep-women -in-world/.

6. Northside Achievement Zone homepage. Accessed at https:// northsideachievement.org/.

7. "NAZ Results Summary: Multigenerational Innovation at Work, 2020," infographic, Northside Achievement Zone. Accessed at https://northside achievement.org/wp-content/uploads/NAZ-Results-FINAL.pdf.

Chapter 2

1. "How Has the Standard of Living for Americans Changed? How Does the Government Help the Disadvantaged?," USA Facts, State of the Union infographic. Accessed at https://usafacts.org/state-of-the-union/standard -living/.

2. "6 Charts That Illustrate the Divide between Rural and Urban America," *PBS Newshour*, March 17, 2017. Accessed at https://www.pbs.org/news hour/nation/six-charts-illustrate-divide-rural-urban-america.

3. Taylor Telford, "Income Inequality in America Is the Highest It's Been Since the Census Bureau Started Tracking It, Data Shows," *Washington Post*, September 26, 2019. Accessed at https://www.washingtonpost.com /business/2019/09/26/income-inequality-america-highest-its-been -since-census-started-tracking-it-data-show/.

4. "Partners for Education," Berea College. Accessed at https://www.berea .edu/pfe/.

5. "King County Census Tracts," Viz Hub Health Data, 2014. Accessed at https://vizhub.healthdata.org/subnational/usa/wa/king-county.

6. Samuel L. Dickman, David U. Himmelstein, and Steffie Woolhandler, "America Equity and Equality in Health 1: Inequality and the Health-Care System," *Lancet* 389 (April 2017): pp. 1431–41. Accessed at https://www. rootcausecoalition.org/wp-content/uploads/2017/04/Inequality -and-the-health-care-system-in-the-USA.pdf.

7. David U. Himmelstein, Robert M. Lawless, Deborah Thorne, Pamela Foohey, Steffie Woolhandler, "Medical Bankruptcy: Still Common Despite the Affordable Care Act," *American Journal of Public Health* 109, vol. 3 (March 2019). Accessed at https://ajph.aphapublications.org/doi/abs /10.2105/AJPH.2018.304901?journalCode=ajph&.

8. John Buntin, "Rural Hospitals Are on Life Support," Governing, April 2014. Accessed at https://www.governing.com/topics/health-human -services/gov-rural-hospitals-on-life-support.html.

9. American Society of Addiction Medicine homepage. Accessed at www .asam.org.

10. "Bill Gates Says US System Produces 'Bogus' Numbers," CNN Coronavirus Town Hall, CNN Business, May 5, 2020. Accessed at https://www.cnn .com/videos/business/2020/05/01/bill-gates-coronavirus-testing -numbers-town-hall-vpx.cnn/video/playlists/cnn-coronavirus-town-hall/.

11. "Confidence in Institutions," Gallup infographic. Accessed at https://news.gallup.com/poll/1597/confidence-institutions.aspx.
12. Pew Research Center. Accessed at pewresearch.org.

Chapter 3

1. Chris Woodford, "Why Do Bridges Collapse," Explain That Stuff. Accessed at https://www.explainthatstuff.com/bridges.html#coll.
2. Pedro Conceição (lead author), "Human Development Report, 2019," United Nations Development Programme. Accessed at http://hdr.undp.org/sites/default/files/hdr2019.pdf.
3. Monica Anderson and Madhumitha Kumar, "Digital Divide Persists Even as Lower-Income Americans Make Gains in Tech Adoption," Pew Research Center, May 7, 2019. Accessed at https://www.pewresearch.org/fact-tank/2019/05/07/digital-divide-persists-even-as-lower-income-americans-make-gains-in-tech-adoption/.
4. Wim Naudé and Paula Nagler, "Is Technological Innovation Making Society More Unequal?" United Nations University, December 21, 2016. Accessed at https://unu.edu/publications/articles/is-technological-innovation-making-society-more-unequal.html.
5. Christoffer Hernaes, "Is Technology Contributing to Increased Inequality," Tech Crunch, March 29, 2017. Accessed at https://techcrunch.com/2017/03/29/is-technology-contributing-to-increased-inequality/.
6. "Tribes by Seth Godin," Samuel Thomas Davies Page. Accessed at https://www.samuelthomasdavies.com/book-summaries/business/tribes/.
7. Aryanna Prasad, "How American Race Relations Shaped Lives of Current, Former Seahawks," *Sports Illustrated*, June 6, 2020. Accessed at https://www.si.com/nfl/seahawks/news/how-american-race-relations-shaped-lives-of-current-former-seahawks.
8. Sam Baker, Alison Snyder, "Coronavirus Hits Poor, Minority Communities Harder," Axios, April 4, 2020. Accessed at https://www.axios.comcoronavirus-cases-deaths-race-income-disparities-unequal-f6fb6977-56a1-4be9-8fdd-844604c677ec.html.

Chapter 4

1. Emily Wadlow, "For Black Lawyers, It's Lonely at the Top," *Washington Post*, October 21, 1979. Accessed at https://www.washingtonpost.com/archive/opinions/1979/10/21/for-black-lawyers-its-lonely-at-the-top/b03f045b-b098-4c07-bc35-75fb98ce0e78/.

Part III

1. Liz Stinson, "China's Sinuous 'Lucky Knot' Bridge Has No Beginning and No End," *Wired*, January 4, 2017. Accessed at https://www.wired.com /2017/01/chinas-sinuous-lucky-knot-bridge-no-beginning-no-end/.

Chapter 5

1. Policy Link homepage. Accessed at https://www.policylink.org/.
2. Alexandra Stevenson and Matthew Goldstein, "Bridgewater's Ray Dalio Spreads His Gospel of 'Radical Transparency,'" *New York Times*, September 8, 2017. Accessed at https://www.nytimes.com/2017/09/08 /business/dealbook/bridgewaters-ray-dalio-spreads-his-gospel-of-radical -transparency.html.
3. Jonathan Haidt and Tobias Rose-Stockwell, "The Dark Psychology of Social Networks," *Atlantic*, December, 2019. Accessed at https://www .theatlantic.com/magazine/archive/2019/12/social-media-democracy /600763/.
4. The Russell Family Foundation homepage. Accessed at www.trff.org.

Chapter 6

1. "Mike Myatt," N2Growth. Accessed at https://www.n2growth.com/team /mike-myatt/.
2. Austa Somvichian-Clausen, "Countries Led by Women Have Fared Better against Coronavirus. Why?" *Hill*, April 18, 2020. Accessed at https:// thehill.com/changing-america/respect/equality/493434-countries-led -by-women-have-fared-better-against.
3. Lauren Wolfe, "Women Leaders Are More Successful in Stopping Coronavirus Than Their Male Counterparts," Women's Media Center, May 16, 2020. Accessed at https://womensmediacenter.com/news -features/women-leaders-are-more-successful-in-stopping-coronavirus -than-their-male-counterparts.
4. Bruce Goldman, "Two Minds: The Cognitive Differences between Men and Women," *Stanford Medicine*, Spring 2017. Accessed at https:// stanmed.stanford.edu/2017spring/how-mens-and-womens-brains-are -different.html.
5. "Mark W. Johnson," Innosight. Accessed at https://www.innosight.com /team_bio/johnson-mark-w/.
6. Vivian Hunt, Dennis Layton, and Sara Prince, "Why Diversity Matters," McKinsey & Company, January 1, 2015. Accessed at https://www.mckinsey .com/business-functions/organization/our-insights/why-diversity -matters.

7. Brittany Karford Rogers, "When Women ~~Don't~~ Speak," *BYU Magazine*, Spring 2020. Accessed at https://magazine.byu.edu/article/when-women-dont-speak/?fbclid=IwAR1bJMW6A3i3AfqhdD3XsL_pB2YWCqjHB8PpxX9tO3K0sLu6dgNHzGq6SeA.

8. Jessica Preece faculty page, BYU FHSS faculty. Accessed at https://fhssfaculty.byu.edu/FacultyPage/jrp68.

9. Social Venture Partners International homepage. Accessed at www.svpi.org.

10. Strive Together homepage. Accessed at https://www.strivetogether.org/.

Chapter 7

1. John Templeton Foundation homepage. Accessed at www.templeton.org.

2. "The Science of Generosity," John Templeton Foundation. Accessed at https://www.templeton.org/discoveries/the-science-of-generosity.

3. Alex Carabi, "Doing vs. Being: The Two Levels of Change," Kodawari Coaching, August 21, 2018. Accessed at http://www.kodawaricoaching.se/blog/doing-vs-being/.

4. "Herb Virgo Grows Life within Keney Park," *Make Hartford Yours*, episode 3, September 1, 2018. Accessed at https://makehartfordyours.wehartford.com/herb-virgo-grows-life-within-hartfords-keney-park/.

5. "What Is Servant Leadership?" Robert K. Greenleaf Center for Servant Leadership, Seton hall University. Accessed at https://www.greenleaf.org/what-is-servant-leadership/.

Chapter 8

1. Project Evident homepage. Accessed at www.projectevident.org.

2. "How We Can Help," Project Evident. Accessed at https://www.projectevident.org/how-we-can-help.

3. Mark Adams, "The Man behind Moneyball: The Billy Beane Story," Domo, February 24, 2015. Accessed at https://www.domo.com/blog/the-man-behind-moneyball-the-billy-beane-story/.

Chapter 9

1. Ashoka homepage. Accessed at www.ashoka.org.

2. Business Roundtable homepage. Accessed at https://www.businessroundtable.org/.

3. David Meyer, "Intel Pledges Ambitious Water-Use Goal by 2030: To Go 'Net-Positive,'" *Fortune*, May 14, 2020. Accessed at https://fortune.com /2020/05/14/intel-water-net-positive-csr-diversity/.
4. Mark R. Kramer, Marc W. Pfitzer, and Helge Mahne, "How Global Leaders Should Think about Solving Our Biggest Problems," *Harvard Business Review*, January 16, 2020. Accessed at https://hbr.org/2020/01/how -global-leaders-should-think-about-solving-our-biggest-problems.

Part IV

1. "Analysis on Unemployment Projects 40-45% Increase in Homelessness This Year," Community Solutions, May 11, 2020. Accessed at https:// community.solutions/analysis-on-unemployment-projects-40-45-increase -in-homelessness-this-year/.
2. "Chattanooga/Southeast Tennessee: Functional Zero Case Study," Community Solutions, January 30, 2020. Accessed at https://community .solutions/stories/case-study-chattanooga-southeast-tennessee-reaches -functional-zero-for-veteran-homelessness/.

Part V

1. Henry Petrovski, "Here's How to Fix America's Crumbling Bridges," The Conversation, November 19, 2014. Accessed at https://theconversation .com/amp/heres-how-to-fix-americas-crumbling-bridges-33781.

Chapter 11

1. "What Works Cities Certification," Bloomberg Philanthropies. Accessed at https://whatworkscities.bloomberg.org/certification/.
2. "Top Foundations Promise Flexible Funding to Grantees in Wake of COVID-19 Crisis," press release, Ford Foundation, March 19, 2020. Accessed at https://www.fordfoundation.org/the-latest/news/top -foundations-pledge-flexible-funding-to-grantees-in-wake-of-covid -19-crisis/.
3. Rima Assi, David Fine, and Kevin Sneader, "The Great Balancing Act: Managing the Coming $30 Trillion Deficit While Restoring Economic Growth," McKinsey & Company, June 16, 2020. Accessed at https://www .mckinsey.com/industries/public-sector/our-insights/the-great -balancing-act-managing-the-coming-30-trillion-dollar-deficit-while -restoring-economic-growth.

Chapter 12

1. Lucas Combos, "Coronavirus Death Was King County Man; More Cases in WA Confirmed," Patch, February 29, 2020. Accessed at https://patch .com/washington/seattle/1-dead-coronavirus-more-cases-washington -officials.
2. Susan Keown, "Tracking the Coronavirus Epidemic from Wuhan to the World," Hutch News Stories, February 25, 2020. Accessed at https://www .fredhutch.org/en/news/center-news/2020/01/2019-ncov-wuhan -coronavirus.html.
3. "A Message from Our CEO," Challenge Seattle, 2019. Accessed at https:// www.challengeseattle.com/our-members.

INDEX

ABOUT THE AUTHOR

If you're out to change the world, author, speaker, and consultant **Paul Shoemaker** is there to connect you to the people, ideas, and organizations that matter. Paul is the founding president of Social Venture Partners International—a global network of thousands of social innovators, entrepreneurs, philanthropists, and business and community leaders that funds and supports social change agents in nearly forty cities and in eight countries. He has also consulted a wide range of organizations to help them define their social change strategies, including UW Medicine, the Ballmer Group, Microsoft, Project Evident, and PolicyLink. With insights from more than twenty years of this unique vantage point, he is the Northwest's leading expert on activating social change agents and a forward-edge thinker on what kind of leadership America will need for the decade ahead.

About the Microsoft Alumni Network Series

THE MICROSOFT ALUMNI NETWORK is a worldwide community of former employees who share a common experience of having worked at Microsoft. Founded in 1995, the Alumni Network is a member organization representing more than fifty thousand alumni in fifty-one countries. The Alumni Network publishing partnership with HarperCollins Leadership represents the broad range of talent that makes up the Microsoft alumni community: entrepreneurs, tech innovators, business professionals, nonprofit leaders, volunteers, and lifelong learners, while shining a light on the meaningful impact that Microsoft's alumni have around the globe.

LISTING OF SERIES BOOKS:

Back to Business: Finding Your Confidence, Embracing Your Skills, and Landing Your Dream Job after a Career Pause
Nancy McSharry Jensen and Sarah Duenwald

Purpose Mindset: How Microsoft Inspires Employees and Alumni to Change the World
Akhtar Badshah

Taking Charge of Change: How Rebuilders Solve Hard Problems
Paul Shoemaker